CALL ME SISTER!

CALL ME SISTER!

District Nursing Tales from the Swinging Sixties

JANE YEADON

BLACK & WHITE PUBLISHING

First published 2013
This edition first published 2014
by Black & White Publishing Ltd
29 Ocean Drive, Edinburgh EH6 6JL

1 3 5 7 9 10 8 6 4 2   14 15 16 17

ISBN: 978 1 84502 738 4

This book is a work of non-fiction, based on the life, experiences and
recollections of Jane Yeadon. In most cases names have been changed
solely to protect the privacy of others. The author has stated to the
publishers that, except in minor respects not affecting the substantial
accuracy of the work, the contents of this book are true.

A CIP catalogue record for this book is available from the British Library.

Typeset by RefineCatch Ltd, Bungay, Suffolk
Printed and bound by Grafica Veneta S. p. A. Italy

To Isean Agam

ACKNOWLEDGEMENTS

Thanks to Black & White Publishing for their unending good humour and guidance, Dr Harry Morgan for his Gaelic expertise, Clio Gray her wise words and Helen Addy for her poem. I must also thank Alister, my Brora wordsmith, and my pals in *for*Words, the Forres writing group.

CONTENTS

Doorstep

Baby shoes, to heels and hob-nails,
I have lifted four generations
through the front door.

Scoured with hard-worn hands,
I roughen women's knees,
but am caressed by their skirts.

Husband and wife sit sharing
a cigarette, the entwined smoke
lengthening the last minute dark.

Imprinted with leavings,
the beginning of every journey,
I am a clear path, a stepping stone.

Helen Addy

1

SHORT RATIONS

It was a bad start to a Monday. The teaspoon count hadn't balanced and a bacon rasher had gone AWOL. Inverness's Raigmore Hospital could be heading for meltdown. With a fresh outbreak of nastiness in my female medical ward and its Sister Gall providing it, my dream of leaving hospital work for district nursing had never looked more attractive. After all, I was a qualified general nurse and midwife; I'd had six months' experience working in a male surgical ward and was now completing another half-year in this one. But even if that was a fair amount of training, I'd yet to come across treatment for a pain in the neck.

Tempted to try throttling, I sat on hands itching to clamp them round Sister Gall's immaculately white collar whilst she used her pointy finger to stab the distance between us. Given our cramped office space, I was lucky she wasn't nearer. Unlucky she was here at all. She wasn't due on duty until the afternoon.

She snapped, 'As staff nurse, it's your responsibility to make sure all equipment is in place and dietary requirements ensured. It's jolly lucky I'm here. I bet you wouldn't have even noticed important things.' She thought for a moment. 'Like spoons and missing food.'

November sleet tracked down the window that rattled in its ill-fitting metal frame. It let in a keen draught whilst giving out onto a complex of brick-built, single-storey buildings. They matched ours but instead of the casualty department which was on our side, there was a maternity unit based at the far end. The distance between the two blocks was tarred and only took a few minutes to walk, less if you could run in rain.

Built as a short-term measure during the Second World War, Raigmore had lasted longer than expected. But even now in the late Sixties a replacement existed only in the imaginations of the optimistic. Still, a teaspoon shortage might highlight the lack of progress.

'Running a hospital's not just about caring, you know. There are other things as important.' Sister Gall's shrill voice raised an octave higher. She was about to retire but wasn't going to go with a whimper.

In a way, I admired her attention to detail. I just wished she was more like the sister in the orthopaedic ward opposite our one. With hair as unlikely a black as Sister Gall's was a definite grey, she was bright, jolly and happy to make up any cutlery shortfall, knowing it would be reciprocated at some point when Sister Gall was off duty. Our wards shared the food trolley, cause of cutlery mix-ups, as well as the separating corridor.

This morning hospital porters were making it a busy road. As they bounced passenger-laden transport bound for theatre, physiotherapy or the X-ray department, their cheerful chat leaked through the ward's heavy entrance doors.

As if offended by it, Sister Gall kicked the office door shut. 'I want a word.' She settled into her chair, jutted her chin, crossed her hands and checked her cap. Nailed into position by an armoury of hairpins, it looked set for all weathers. My inner barometer diagnosed dropping mercury with a distinct probability of an imminent storm.

She drew breath. 'That place opposite,' she thumb-pointed, 'is full of folk who, like you, have taken up this daft new sport. I expect you were doing it this weekend too. *Skiing!*' She spat the word out. 'Now, just think of that ward. I know it's full of patients with broken bones. I'm only here this morning because I thought you might easily have become one of them, and then I'd have to operate with even more of a staff shortage.'

Shaking her head in bewilderment, she flicked open the Kardex, a patients' record folder, and tapped a stubby finger against a patient's name. 'And it's lucky I did. There was bacon sent from the kitchens for Mrs Mackay, but according to her she hasn't had any breakfast.'

I went for a cool, 'I didn't give it to her because of her morning sickness. She'd just have brought it back up.'

Casting a disparaging look at the Aberdeen Training School badge pinned on my apron, Sister Gall fingered her own. It proved she'd trained at Raigmore, something she never failed to point out was superior to any other training hospital. 'Our patient's a diabetic,' she said, 'and once she'd got over that sickness nonsense, she could have had that bacon. We'd just have reheated it.'

I thought about our pale and retching patient. I'd been surprised she wasn't in the maternity part of the hospital. Maybe they'd no staff. Maybe all their midwives had gone skiing and were stuck, injured or lost in the wild fastnesses of the Cairngorms, and maybe this wasn't a good time to say so.

'Right!' I hoped my tone conveyed dignity and resolve. 'I'll go and make her a cup of tea and see if she can keep down some toast.'

But Sister Gall wasn't going to give up. She barked, 'She should have that bacon to make sure she's getting the right number of calories.'

Exasperated, I went for broke. 'Well, I threw it out.'

Her eyes narrowed and she looked crafty. 'No you didn't. I checked the bins and it's not there and neither is the spoon.'

Crikey! She was hell bent on discovery.

Actually, I'd left the bacon on a plate in the ward kitchen. Remembering the rhythmic chewing of Mhairi, the ward maid, shortly after I'd told her Mrs Mackay would never eat it, I settled back in my chair and opted for honesty. Facing Sister Gall directly, I said, 'Well, I don't know where it is . . . now.'

With timing a second short of miraculous, the ward resident doctor stuck his head round the door. 'Ah! Sister,' he said. 'Good to see you. I'm a bit concerned about Mrs Mackay. Looks a bit pale to me. Could you come and have a look?'

'I'm not supposed to be here.' Sister Gall was coy. 'But as you're new here and if it puts your mind to rest, certainly. I'm always ready to help.'

Our doctor was tall and thin with a white coat so starched it made him look like a long pharmaceutically-wrapped parcel. Little Sister Gall in blue, resembling someone bundled into a square one, went off after him, having to hurry to catch up. I grabbed the chance to nip into the kitchen.

'*Muirst!*' ('Murder!') Mhairi's Gaelic was as accurate as the mouthful of tea she aimed into the sink. 'Is she still around? She was here going through the bins. I'd to keep well away from her. She's got a nose like a bloodhound. For a moment I thought she might pass a tube down my throat to prove her suspicious wee mind. Has she not got a home to go to?'

'The Old Folks' one wouldn't take her,' I said, too irritated to be loyal. 'Just don't breathe near her, and see if you can get a spoon from over the way. Otherwise we'll never hear the end of it.'

A student nurse and auxiliary were also on duty. I found them in the sluice discussing the Saturday night dance at the Caley, a popular hotel in town.

'Loads of talent,' said Student Nurse Black, whose name belied her blonde hair. 'I was never off the floor. It was just great.' She eyed me with kindly curiosity. 'Have you a boyfriend, Staffie?'

I thought about David, newly graduated and working as a hotel manager in Glasgow. He made me laugh, shared my Morayshire background and had blue eyes that could have melted my heart, was it not so set on becoming a district nurse.

'No,' I said, 'but I bet you've plenty. You could give me some of your spares.'

She laughed. She was bonny with a bubbly personality that made her an engaging addition to the staff. She had a soft voice, which seemed alien in the clinical surroundings of the sluice, and she also turned out to have a flair for floral art. Even Sister Gall seemed to appreciate a gift that brought life and colour to our spare quarters, based, as they were, in buildings one step up from Nissen huts.

'Ach, right enough. I mind the days,' sighed the auxiliary, emptying a bedpan and turning on a tap.

Sister Gall was obviously out of earshot, otherwise they wouldn't have been having such a delightful conversation. Notwithstanding the Caley's attractions, they seemed clear as to their duties so I left them and went to check on Mrs Mackay.

Unlike some of the wards with their long stretch, ours was broken up into six-bedded units. These gave increased privacy, but Mrs Mackay, with her substantial bump and youth, looked out of place amongst the other patients, many of whom were old and determinedly snoring.

Soon, I thought, we'll be getting them out of bed. They won't want that, and who could blame them? Sitting in a draughty corner, looking at the ward's green-painted brick walls didn't hold much in the way of improved prospects, even if it shifted pressure off their bums and helped prevent bedsores.

Mrs Mackay sat up in bed and punched her pillows. 'I'm such a nuisance,' she declared, pushing back a tangled rope of black hair. 'Sister Gall was cross I couldn't eat my breakfast, but I just can't face anything greasy first thing in the morning. I did tell her but she wasn't for listening. She was in right bad tune. I hope you didn't get into any trouble?'

'No, no. She's just anxious to get your diabetes under control. But maybe you could eat a slice of toast now, and what about a cup of tea?'

'Oooh!' She winced and put her hand over her bump.

'You sore?'

She shook her head. 'Just a wee twinge.'

I put my hand on her stomach and felt it tighten under my touch. 'Mmm. Tell you what, you have a go at some tea and toast. I'll get someone to make it for you.'

She looked anxious. 'Anything wrong? With this being a first, I don't know what to expect, but Nurse,' she said, grasping my arm in a surprisingly firm grip for someone so gentle and undemanding, 'it's not due until the end of next month.'

'Did Doctor or Sister examine you?'

'Well, they took a urine sample and my pulse, but now you've got me worried about the baby. Next thing it'll be my blood pressure.' Mrs Mackay sighed and bit her lip. There was a sheen of sweat on her forehead. Maybe she was hypoglycaemic. Too much insulin could do that. Oh dear! She definitely needed something to eat.

A year ago I'd qualified as a midwife in Belfast. The Royal Maternity Hospital's work was so specialised a normal delivery was a surprise. The training had been hard work, with plenty drama. I'd thought I'd have a break from it so the last thing I expected in a medical ward was this.

I said, 'I'm sure everything's fine, but I'll come back in a minute and have a wee look. It's maybe worth checking.'

I needed to see Mrs Mackay's notes and was so sure Sister Gall had gone, it was a surprise finding her in the office mulling over them with the doctor. Frowning, she looked up. 'Shouldn't you be dressing that bedsore?'

So much for patient care and identity! I wondered if nursing for as long as she had had made her forget she was there because of patients. Maybe over a period of time in the same hospital surroundings you could be so taken over by inventories you could become lost to patients' needs. I hoped I'd never lose sight of the fact that they had names, and the one with the bedsore was Miss Caird.

She was an old lady who lived in an isolated house in an Inverness-shire glen. Noticing a lack of lights in the home, a neighbour had checked on her. When she found her in bed, dehydrated, emaciated and with a foul-smelling bedsore, she immediately sought medical help. Miss Caird was confused, but nobody was sure if that was due to her present state or because she might already have dementia.

'She's never been one for company and she's seemed to be getting even worse. Lately it's got so she wouldn't allow anyone near the place,' explained the neighbour who'd found Miss Caird. Glancing round the ward, she added, 'And she'd never have been here if she'd been conscious. She'll no like it here at all at all.'

Even if she was screened off and the other patients spoke quietly, how could she? This must be a planet away from her own world, where the elements prevailed. Now, under our care and a ceiling of peeling plaster, she lay quiet and undemanding. Only a faint gleam in the faded blue of her eyes when anyone spoke to her showed she had an awareness of sorts.

Her infected sore demanded the sort of attention which made it all too easy to forget the sufferer. I understood why a trained member of staff with a stomach less queasy than a student's should have to deal with this, but not why Sister Gall always made herself exempt. Still, she was supposed to be off duty at the moment and I *was* meant to be in charge.

I knew the dressing needed to be done, but it would take time, our most limited commodity. Reckoning our pregnant patient was a priority, I persevered with my audience. 'I'm not sure Mrs Mackay's contractions are Braxton Hicks. They're usually painless, but I think she's feeling these ones.'

Sister Gall and the doctor looked puzzled, so I continued. 'We wouldn't want to risk a delivery here, especially with a diabetic.'

Sister Gall shuffled some papers in exasperation. 'Instead of frittering away your time, I suggest you go and do that dressing as I told you to do ten minutes ago. Mrs Mackay was fine when we saw her, wasn't she, Doctor?'

The doctor, looking worried, nodded. 'Of course, I'm not up so much on midwifery. Unless we wanted to specialise in it, our training didn't cover it in great detail. Maybe if Nurse Macpherson's a trained midwife, we should be listening to her.'

'What?' Sister Gall was shocked. 'Mrs Mackay's here to have her diabetes stabilised, not to have a baby, and Nurse Macpherson's here as a staff nurse in a medical ward. Good gracious! I've never heard the like. Anyway, the diabetic consultant's coming in this morning. He'll know best.'

'Will he be coming soon?' I wondered aloud.

'Soon enough. Now just get on with the other work. There's a whole ward to run.'

'Yes, Sister.'

Miss Caird lay so still that for a moment I thought she might be dead, but her eyelids fluttered when I touched her cheek. 'I'm coming to see you soon,' I whispered. 'I've just a wee worry on at the moment.'

I got back to Mrs Mackay. She was now looking so uncomfortable that I began to really fret.

'Is your tummy tightening regularly?' I asked, noting the unfinished tea and half-eaten toast.

'Everything's fine, isn't it?'

'Oh, just dandy. But just to be sure, let's have a look at you.'

A quick examination was enough. And enough was enough. Holding out her dressing gown and slippers, I said, 'Come on, Mrs Mackay, you climb into these whilst I get a wheelchair. We're going on a trip and it's from here to Maternity.'

2

ROSEMARY FOR REMEMBRANCE

I was in such a hurry to get Mrs Mackay wheelchaired over to Maternity, I nearly ran over Sister Gall. She must have heard the sound of the racing wheels because she shot out of the office. She looked furious.

'Can't stop,' I said, knowing that if I did, things could become undignified. I'd just have to deal with her when I came back. Right now, that wasn't a priority. Certain that our patient was in labour, I knew that, once delivered, her baby would need special care and probably in an incubator. When I got back, and reasoning that this might strike a chord, I'd say to Sister Gall, 'And as far as I'm aware, that's not part of our ward's inventory.'

Between silently practising the lines and assuring Mrs Mackay that we hadn't quite reached the sound barrier break point, we arrived at the Maternity Unit. It had been a long sprint and by the time I handed over my charge, I was quite out of breath. Struggling to get it back before returning to Medical, I rehearsed my put-down lines but could have saved myself the bother. My senior had stomped off, saying she'd had enough for one morning. We'd see her in the afternoon.

So, now and having the time, I attended to Miss Caird. As I dressed a dreadful sore that demanded every skill I could muster, I packed the foul-smelling space where there had once been flesh.

I looked for some sign of healing; it'd be a gauge on her health. There was none. Any point of contact now seemed to bruise her skin whilst, under its translucence, her veins mapped out their blue, tortuous routes.

A simple arrangement of flowers stood in a vase nearby. Nurse Black must have put them there, as well as provided the tartan ribbon tying back Miss Caird's lank grey hair. I feared it was too late for her to notice those small kindnesses. With her weak pulse and shallow breathing, she seemed to be drifting downwards and ever faster from us.

I wished I knew more about her. There were no clues from the few possessions stored in the old-fashioned metal locker parked beside her bed. Her neighbour had brought them in and she was her only, but occasional, visitor. She knew little other than what she'd previously told us.

'Private and proud,' she'd reiterated, shaking her head. 'Private and proud.'

Aware that even if Miss Caird seemed far away, she might still hear things going on around her, I settled for a one-way conversation. 'One of our patients has gone over to Maternity. I think she was a bit surprised. You see, her baby isn't due for a while. We've just to hope everything will be fine.'

Although there was no response, I sensed she was listening, so I carried on. 'They're awful busy over there so I don't suppose they'll have time to let us know how she's getting on. But when I go off duty I'll nip along to Maternity, find out, and then I'll come back and tell you.'

It didn't take that long.

Sister Gall made her official return, looking as if she'd been caught in the rain. She was drying her spectacles whilst her cap had little blotches on it, making it look a little less starchy. It was even a little askew. Replacing her spectacles but avoiding eye contact, she sounded subdued as she said, 'I went over to check on Mrs Mackay before coming on duty. You were right. She was in labour.' She sighed gustily. 'She's had her baby and it's a girl.'

'And how are they?'

'She's OK. Worried about the baby, of course. I went to see it. It looks too big to be in an incubator.' Referring to the baby as an 'it' seemed to give Sister Gall slight satisfaction. She was beginning to pick up speed. 'Makes you wonder if they know what they're doing over there.'

I thought I might say diabetic mothers' babies were often big and would soon lose the extra fluid they carried and return to a more normal weight. Considering Sister Gall's recent learning curve, I decided that although she hadn't done midwifery training herself, she'd probably had enough for one day and she'd appreciate a return to familiar ground.

'I'm sure they'll both be fine, but actually I'm more worried about Miss Caird. She's really going downhill.'

Like a circus horse smelling sawdust, Sister Gall perked up. She sat up straight and lifted her chin. 'Right. You go back, keep an eye on her and I'll tell the doctor. We can't have her suffering.' Already she was on the phone.

I was right to be anxious. Our patient had become flushed, restless and was muttering in a different language. It could be Gaelic. I couldn't understand it but Mhairi probably would. While waiting for the doctor, I decided to ask her.

She looked surprised but pleased. '*Gu deibhinin* (certainly), it's my native tongue!' she said, drying her hands and coming with me. 'It's when I speak from the heart.'

I could see that. After listening closely to Miss Caird and murmuring back some Gaelic words, she translated. 'She says she's going to die.' With an awkward hand, she soothed Miss

Caird's brow. 'I've told her to be brave and she's in good hands, but look, Staff, she's frightened.' She pointed to tears streaming down Miss Caird's withered cheeks.

I felt awful. I should have realised she was in all probability a native Gaelic speaker. No wonder communication was poor. Now it seemed time was moving too fast for me to make up for a lost opportunity. She probably never understood a word I was saying. Settling for the next best thing, I whispered to my interpreter, 'Mhairi, could you tell her about Mrs Mackay and her having a baby and we're sure everything's going to be all right.'

The ward maid bent down and relayed the message. It sounded like a lullaby. The only sign that Miss Caird might have heard was her faint muttering. Now the other patients, never loud at the best of times, fell silent. It was as if they were all holding their breath and listening.

Then, Sister Gall's stubby fingers pulled back the surrounding screens, their rail-fastenings rattle, breaking the silence. One look at our patient and after a brief exchange of glances with the doctor, she took over.

'Right, Miss Caird, It's a bit busy round here and you need plenty rest and something to help your pain, so we're going to move you into the wee room opposite my office. It'll be easier to keep an eye on you there.' Grasping the rail at the head of the bed, she said, 'Right, Doctor, you take the other end, and, Staff,' she gave me a nod, 'you can get on with the rest of the work.'

With the screening curtains swept back and Miss Caird moved out, the ward's other patients moved into a chattier mode. Later that day, a stroke victim would fill the space left by Miss Caird. She'd be surrounded by an anxious family who were either thronging every corner or jamming the hospital telephone line demanding a progress report. Sister Gall found them a pain and a lot more difficult than the care of Miss Caird. But soon that wouldn't be needed either and the room opposite the office was emptied. One day, as quietly as she had come, Miss Caird drifted away.

It's a sad fact but all nurses have to learn to cope with death. This would be Nurse Black's first one. I supposed that I'd be the one helping her handle it, but Sister Gall shook her head. She said, 'I'll take her and show her what to do, but it's a traumatic enough experience without her having to see that awful sore. Will you make sure it's covered before we start? She's a good wee nurse and we don't want to lose her.'

Was it my imagination or was there a slight softening in Sister Gall's steely approach? Her consideration was as unexpected as was the tone of the dressings request. Afterwards, Nurse Black's reaction to the experience was unexpected as well.

She was in the sluice putting fresh water into a vase of flowers. Concentrating on drying the base, she mused, 'Don't you worry, I'm fine, Staffie. And you know, I was dreading dressing a dead body and I certainly didn't expected Old Gallstone to be anything but practical, business-like and totally uncaring.' She sniffed hard then continued. 'And of course Miss Caird was a very private person. But Sister Gall dealt with her as if she was still alive and gave her the respect and dignity I'm sure she'd have wanted. Honestly, she made the whole business seem easy but right. *And she let me use rosemary*,' the young student finished with a note of triumph. 'After I told her it was a herb for remembrance she let me weave a sprig of it through Miss Caird's fingers. It made them look almost alive. I felt it was a good way of saying goodbye. What d'you think, Staff?'

Linking her arm in mine and handing her a tissue, I said, 'I can't think of a better way of marking your care. It shows that someone we thought unknown who kept herself to herself will never be forgotten. And I'll never forget you for your tribute.'

3

A NEW ADVENTURE

'So, you'll be off skiing, I suppose?'

Sister Gall was doing her best. We were in the office and after giving her the handover report I had a day off. Since Mrs Mackay's transfer to Maternity, the ward sister had softened a bit, at least enough to consider her staff might have a life outwith food calorie and cutlery counts. She had even begun to trust me to run the ward when she was off duty.

Toning down the criticism she'd so easily given before must have been difficult. It would be a shame for me to lose this goodwill, but it was sure to go if I were to tell her I'd applied for a district nursing job in Ross-shire. I'd be spending my day off having an interview in the county's headquarters which were in Dingwall, twenty miles north of Inverness.

My sister Elizabeth and I had two maiden aunts who used to live there. When we were on our summer holiday staying with our granny in Nairn, the highlight was to visit them. I don't know why we never went by train. It would have been possible, and quicker. Maybe Granny's Calvinistic spirit rejected the idea of ease, leading her to declare with exasperation, 'You're both such poor travellers. I hope you can make it at least as far as Inverness without actually being actually sick. When we change buses there, you'll get a break. That sometimes helps.'

What she actually meant was that puking into a paper bag was one thing, but holding on to allow a timely sprint to the bus stop toilet showed fortitude – and a paper bag saved for the second half of the journey. Break or not, the journey seemed to last forever. When we did eventually arrive at our aunts' house, we were queasy. We smelt of petrol and cigarette smoke, but their welcome was absolute, if dangerous.

'Come in, come in!' They'd cry, throwing open their thin little arms. Then Nanny, the eldest, would shepherd us towards, then make us sit down at a small, round and very unstable table. Covered in an exquisitely hand-embroidered linen tablecloth, it would be groaning with food. 'You must all be starving. Look! We've had a lovely morning preparing this. We've even made sausage rolls 'cos we know what wee lassies like, don't we, Jessie?'

'Yes. Lemonade too, and after everything's been scoffed, we'll have a wee concert. Your granny tells us you're wonderful dancers.'

With a sly look at this unexpected promoter of our talents, Nanny put in, 'Singers too.'

She was so enthusiastic we could only oblige. Well into her spinsterhood, perhaps Nanny was looking for some recognisable genetic imprint in us. It certainly wasn't in looks, for neither aunt had my red hair and freckles nor Elizabeth's dark curly hair. Instead, tortoiseshell-backed hair clasps held back faded blonde hair from their pale serene faces.

The aunts scratched a living teaching country dancing and were good teachers, accustomed to the space of the halls where they taught. Bothered by stage fright and shyness, my sister pointed out the limitations of their minute sitting room.

'Och don't be shy,' encouraged Nanny. 'Look, you. We'll move the table. You're not big girls. We're sure you'll manage. Just don't dance too near the glass cabinet.'

With Jessie playing the piano and Nanny providing illustrative footwork on the neatest and lightest of pins, we were inspired to dance and warble. Under praise heaped on by two gentle souls, schooled in tact, we grew cocky. We leapt imaginatively and ever higher until the glass cabinet ornaments put in a protest.

Catching the aunts' anxiety, Granny rose. 'Time to go,' she said. 'Come along, girls. Getting back to Inverness itself, never mind Nairn, takes time.'

She was right then, but now as I drove my Hillman Imp out of Inverness, the way seemed familiar but shorter. The road still wound its way along the Beauly Firth with the railway track making the occasional snaking companion alongside, whilst the sea waves still left old lace frills on the shore. In the distance seabirds floated in a line on the water, looking like a musical score.

The Rosemarkie transmitter was clearly visible on the skyline. When we were growing up on an upland Morayshire farm, we had a clear view of the Moray Firth. The sudden appearance in 1957 of an eye like a Cyclops on it astonished us, particularly as it turned out to belong to a transmitter clearing snow from our telly screens. As it was responsible for such a miraculous effect, I hoped that without the sophistication of a car radio, it would also help my tranny to work. I switched it on, hoping it would take my mind off interview anxiety.

'You can't always get what you want,' sang The Rolling Stones. It was a bit different from 'How much is that doggy in the window?', a song my aunts swore was their favourite tune.

'We could sing it again,' I'd volunteered, eager for even more praise.

'No, don't! It was so good the first time, you couldn't better it,' said Granny, fumbling with her hearing aid.

I bet she'd have been surprised that I'd actually found such a doggie in Dingwall. And in a window! Driving into the county headquarters car park, I glimpsed a small black one sitting in the front of a Morris Minor already there. It watched with cocked ears as the driver climbed out. She wore a district nurse's uniform and had the competent look of someone who if you asked for directions would give them clearly and concisely. The pillbox hat worn at a jaunty angle and the fish net stockings suggested, however, that there was more to her than map reading.

'You mind the car now, Jomo,' she said, shutting the car door. Right away, the little dog jumped into her seat and, putting paws on the steering wheel, looked out of the window with the enquiring eye of a professor. The car horn sounded once. Looking round and evidently satisfied with what he saw, he settled down.

She'd such a friendly, open way. I felt I could ask the question.

'Jomo?'

'Kenyatta, of course,' she replied. 'It had to be, with his colour and wee beard.' She took in my suit, chosen because of its restrained colour and hem length, and smiled. Tightening her blue gabardine coat against the chilly November wind snarling about us, she said, 'And I suppose you're here for your interview? Come on, I'll take you to Miss Macleod. She said you'd be coming.'

The everyday sounds of a council department were very different from those of a hospital, and whilst the corridor floor had the same gleam (proving the industry of dedicated polishers), the place felt warm, relaxed and welcoming.

I glimpsed staff through half-open doors and heard their easy chat. Amongst the notices on the doors, one said 'Sanitary Inspectors' and 'Architects'. It looked an unusual combination but the chaps lolling over their desks seemed to be sharing banter in an atmosphere conducive to a stress-free day.

The proximity of Medical Officer of Health to Superintendent of Nursing made more sense. My companion tapped on a nameplate, then opened the door.

18

'Morning, Miss Macleod. I've someone here I know you're expecting,' she said.

'Come in, come in.' Miss Macleod got up a from behind a mighty desk she shared with a Bakelite telephone and a black Conway Stewart fountain pen lying beside a rocking blotter. She was tall and her straight skirt was shorter than mine, her shoes a lot less sensible. She was elegant, friendly even. She stretched out a lily-white hand, so smooth it would have scandalised Sister Gall.

'You've met Sister Shiach, I see.' She gave my companion an approving nod. 'She takes all our new members of staff for a few weeks. Shows them the ropes and, I have to say, she's also Dingwall's finest asset.'

Sister Shiach waved a dismissive hand. 'Ach, away with you. There's a few mums'll no be saying that when I tell them their bairns have lice. I'm here to get some orange juice and hair shampoo for them. See if that stops them showing me the door.' She tapped her hat as if to illustrate a thinking moment, then with a flash of strong-looking teeth, reversed out.

Miss Macleod sat down again. She leant against the navy-blue suit jacket slung across the back of her chair. She stretched her arms out so that she could spread her fingers on the desk.

'You're young to want to be a district nursing *sister*.'

Remembering the eighteen-year-old Nurse Black's view that the next step for a twenty-three-year-old was hospitalisation in a geriatric ward, I was pleased about the youth bit but a little surprised at the sister emphasis. Eliminating 'nurse' from my vocabulary, I went for a cautious, 'I've always wanted to be one.'

'I've read your application. It's come at a good time. We've actually got a vacancy for a relief sister.' She tapped her fingers together in an approving sort of way. 'And your qualifications seem suitable. I'm anxious to give the district nursing service a

19

more youthful profile. You'll have to go for the district nurse training, of course, but we'll send you on the course if we take you on and when I see how you do.'

She frowned, straightened her shoulders then fixed me with a stern look. 'Of course, too many people don't think of us as highly trained professionals. They have a problem thinking of us as anything else but nurses when we have every right to be addressed as "Sisters."' She rapped the desk. '"Sisters!"'

Behind the classy spectacles her eyes were shrewd as she asked, 'But always wanting to be a district nursing sister isn't quite enough, so, could you expand on your reason for wanting to be one?'

I thought about my mother's friend, Nurse Dallas. Her opinions and homespun philosophies were given great respect. She had a house, a hat that could hide bad hair days, a car, a dog, and people, including my strong and independently minded mother, took her advice. Who wouldn't want that? She was simply named after the parish she served. I never knew her real name. But maybe the Dallas bit as much as the Nurse title would offend Miss Macleod. It'd be safer telling her about Miss Caird.

'We need hospitals,' I began, stating the obvious, but I had to start somewhere, 'and by the time one lady came to the ward I work in, she couldn't have been left at home. The trouble was, she was such a hermit, the hospital environment with all its staff must have been a nightmare to her. She was really ill before she was admitted and by the time she got to us she was past being able to make any decisions.'

I paused for a moment, hoping I was getting the right pitch. 'But had she a choice, I imagine she'd have wanted to die at home. As it was, she was dressed in starched hospital gowns, surrounded by strange sounds and people who didn't speak her language. It would have been so much kinder if somebody had been able to care for her, much earlier and at home.' I bent my head, remembering that lost chance. 'And I'd like to be part of a service that helps that to happen. Really worthwhile work.'

'And can you speak Gaelic?' Miss Macleod, with her Edinburgh accent, sounded genuinely interested.

'No. But there was a staff member in the ward who did. I'd put that down to local knowledge and I would imagine that if your nursing sisters don't know something, they'll know someone in their district who does.'

The sound of laughter floated into the room. Miss Macleod got up, I thought to stop it, but she just said, 'Yes. Hospitals have their place it's true, but care can't be bettered if it's delivered in a home environment by appropriately trained staff who know what else is going on in the patient's life.' She smiled, smoothed already smooth hair, checked it in the wall mirror as she passed, then heading for the door, said, 'Now, I'll take you to meet Dr Duncan. He's our Medical Officer of Health. We work closely and I always involve him in staff matters. Come along.'

Dr Duncan's office had papers scattered all over the place. The Sellotape fixing some to the walls was curling and yellowing with age. The man himself was smart in a three-piece grey suit. He had the courteous manner of someone accustomed to dealing with the public but with a slightly distracted air, as if waiting for a message.

I noticed an exchanged nod just as introductions were made. Then, patting his waistcoat, he leant over his desk and extended his hand. His accent told me he came from the east coast. 'I hear you did your general training in Aberdeen. A good medical school there too.' He stretched his neck as he adjusted a university tie. 'And I imagine you'd have seen life doing your midwifery training in Belfast.'

I nodded, steeling myself for a question that might well decide my future. There was a pause whilst he gazed at a slightly askew health promotion poster. It must have been important; it had each corner pinned to the wall. Then slowly and as if it was the most searching question he could think up, he said, 'So when do you think you could start?'

4

TRAVELLERS' PROBLEMS

I told Sister Gall about the job and that I'd be starting at the beginning of January.

'Not a good time. You'll have trouble on the roads,' she said, looking out of the window and getting a grim satisfaction from a wintry scene. 'See, it's snowing already. You'll get lost in the first drift.'

Feeling bound to defend myself, I followed her to the sluice where we were due a stock count. I said, 'But I'll be with a Sister Shiach for the first few weeks, and she's very experienced. They mightn't miss me but I think they'd notice if she got lost.'

She was sour. 'Sister indeed! They used to be happy being just called nurses. Anyway, I can't think why you're going to do district. It's a waste of a good nurse. I'd have thought with me retiring you might have applied for the job.' She had to go on tiptoe to count the bottles lined up on the sluice shelf.

'We'll need four more bottles of disinfectant.' She thrust an order form at me. 'See to it, will you? I've plenty other things to do. Dingwall's full of tinkers but there's one less just now and she's in our ward. Dusty Williamson needs an eye kept on her. She could have a fit at any moment.' She clicked her teeth. 'If only she'd taken her epilepsy medication she wouldn't *be* in hospital. She could be annoying *Sister* Shiach instead.'

I thought it a shame Sister Gall didn't have the gentle spirit of my aunts whose view on tinkers had been entirely different.

'We look forward to a visit from the travelling people and we always buy their bonny straw baskets,' Nanny had explained. 'We don't really need any but they make such lovely presents. The poor souls need the money and, of course, we're always needing clothes pegs so we get them too.'

'And that's theirs,' Jessie said, pointing to the glass cabinet where a matching cup and saucer decorated with roses sat on a shelf by itself. 'We keep it 'specially for them. They always laugh when they see it. We'd give them another but they insist on sharing that one. We hope they like taking tea out of it. We try to make it a special occasion for them. They can't get many treats.'

Both aunts were now gone but I hoped that there was still that sort of kindness in Dingwall, if not immediately apparent in the sluice. 'Humph!' said Sister Gall, moving out of it. 'Tinks!'

The ward resident also had a view on my move: less judgemental, but no more encouraging. He said, 'Would you not think of doing intensive care? There's a job coming up in that department. I think you'd be good at that.'

'I'd take that as a compliment if I didn't get the feeling you think I'm best at dealing with unconscious folk.'

He was quick to reply, 'No, no. It's just that I think you'd be good at meeting the challenge.'

'And I've just got a job I've always wanted to do and a house,' I said, 'so I can't think what could be better.'

'You've maybe got a point,' said the recently married doctor suddenly, and in a heart-felt way. 'Raigmore's hospital staff quarters are pretty basic. My wife feels she's sharing her life with every other person in the block.'

Nurse Black thought that wouldn't be so bad. 'Won't you find it scary living on your own?' she asked.

24

I was confident. 'District nurses' houses are usually at the heart of the community, so it's not as if I'll be stuck at the back of beyond and on my own.' I warmed to my theme. 'And I'll be in lots of different places if I'm doing holiday relief. It'll give me a great way to see Ross-shire. Anyway, I was brought up on a hill farm so I'm used to and love open spaces.'

Life without the Caley dances was plainly an anathema to my young colleague. 'But what'll you do for a social life?'

'I'll get the bright lights in Edinburgh. At some point, and if I'm a good girl, I'll get to go and do the district nursing course there.'

'Staff Nurse!' Sister Gall called. 'Will you stop that gassing and get a spatula? Dusty's off again.'

Our patient was having a full-blown epileptic fit. With her rolling eyes and jerking, convulsive movements, she looked like a marionette controlled by some vicious puppeteer. In her screened-off bed, she was at risk of throwing herself beyond its contained space.

We eased the wooden spatula into her frothing mouth. 'That'll stop her biting her tongue,' said Sister Gall, 'but these grand mal fits can't be doing her any good. Keep an eye on her. If this lasts much longer, she'll need to be seen by the consultant – and get Nurse Black to help you change the bed. I'll bet Dusty's been incontinent.' She bustled off, calling back, 'And I'll finish the list. Think we'll need another bottle of disinfectant.'

Dusty's movements slowly relaxed. Recovering consciousness, she spat out the spatula.

'I was away again, then?' she said in a matter-of-fact way. 'Och but those fits wear me out!' She yawned, showing black tusks that were the remnants of her teeth and a blight in a face, with its skin so fine it looked as if it was made of porcelain.

'Sister Gall's no best pleased I forget to take my pills. Anyway, I canna always afford them or even get to a chemist. And when I'm out on the road, it's easy to lose time. Sometimes I don't even notice a day going by. Anyway I hate the damn things.' She sighed and gazed out of the window. 'You don't think I'll be here long do you?'

Her brother would occasionally visit. The last time I saw him I heard him say, 'You'll no get out if you dinna have an address, and you ken you canna sign yourself out. You canna write an' neither can I.' He was as thin as his sister and had the same bright red hair. But whilst Dusty's flamed round her face, his clung in tight curls on top of his head. He looked ill at ease and out of place with his ragged clothes. His mud-spattered boots were so big he could hardly hide them under his chair. Unlike Dusty, however, his teeth shone even and white in a sunburnt face.

Awkwardly patting her hand, he smiled and said, 'Just tell the doctors you're going to Dingwall. Like you usually do. That seems to suit them. Anyway, that's where our folk are.' After he visited, the smell of wood smoke lingered in a ward I was soon to leave.

When it came to then, Sister Gall, to my surprise, had organised a little tea party. I nearly asked for a bacon sandwich. Instead we had Penguin biscuits and drank strong tea out of the Pyrex cups from the tea set I'd been gifted.

'You tell me you'll be based in Conon Bridge. That's near Dingwall and of course it's where Dusty *said* she'd be going.' Sister Gall sounded doubtful. 'You never know, you might just meet her and then you could ask her to pop in and visit you.' She swung a cup as if giving a toast, then with just a touch of mischief, she added, 'And if she does, you might find one of these'll come in handy. Just don't bother with the saucer.'

5

SISTER SHIACH
SHOWS THE WAY

I never did see Dusty but I was reminded of her brother not long after starting my apprenticeship with Sister Shiach. On a late afternoon in January, she was driving us along a street of Dingwall council houses. One had a chimney puffing out wood smoke that, despite the closed windows, crept in to fill the car with the familiar smell that Dusty's brother brought with him when visiting her.

Jomo was in his usual place, riding shotgun in the front of the car, whilst I was crammed into the back. I hoped the Williamsons were, despite their wandering ways, somewhere more comfortable. However, accompanying Sister Shiach had other attractions.

'I feel like the Duke of Edinburgh,' I joked. 'We can't go anywhere but people are waving and smiling at you. Look at that old man. He's just got off his bike to wave to you.'

Slowing down to nod and smile back, she said, 'Oh dear. I'm thinking he can hardly afford to be out, never mind on his bike. At least he got off it. He's getting so doddery these days, he could easily have fallen under my car wheels.' She furrowed her brow and glanced at me in her mirror. 'D'you think he looks a bit peely-wally? I'd say he looks a bit anaemic. Maybe I should have a word with the doc.'

Thinking these car journeys were a bit like a ward round and might explain Sister Shiach's erratic driving style, I said, 'You must know everybody.'

She laughed and shrugged. 'Well, folk know us by the Morris Minors, they're such a terrible colour. Miss Macleod seems to think they tone in with the uniform!' She snorted. 'Personally, I'd love something of my own choice and bigger. I'm working on her to see if we can get to buy our own.'

I persevered. 'Well, I think folk'll still recognise you, car colour or not.'

She waved a deprecating hand. 'If they do, it's only because I've been here such a long time. You know, I sometimes think that if I haven't seen them at one end of their lives I'll be around for the other. I'm not sure if I'm seen as all that helpful either.' She sighed. 'For instance, I've been a right pain in the proverbial to the mum we're going to see. I'd forgotten she's gone from living in a van to moving to a house. I've had to learn to make allowances for her that I mightn't consider having for other patients. There's been a lot of learning for both of us.'

We'd spent the mornings visiting patients who needed essential nursing care. I was always impressed by my advisor's kind, warm approach and easy relationship with her patients. If I can copy her, I thought, I'll be all right. The afternoons, however, were generally spent on post-natal and health visiting, and they were more daunting from my point of view.

'But I haven't got health visitor qualifications,' I'd protested at the outset.

Sister Shiach had been reassuring. 'Neither have some of the other girls,' she said. 'You'll eventually need to get yours. The course takes a year. But the fact of the matter is that in this neck of the woods, we don't have that many bairns under school age and it's not that difficult to spot problems. Anyway, it's really a matter of common sense and we all work closely with the doctors *and* you'll have got to know the family through your ante and post-natal care.' She'd sounded sanguine.

Now, sharing the back of the car with an assortment of equipment, I considered her remarks. A card-holding box sat on top of some spare sheets, continence aids and a nursing bag. Added to this was a carrier bag full of children's clothes with a navy blue duffle coat spread over it. Common sense told me Sister Shiach was in charge.

She gestured with her thumb towards the clothes bag. 'Grab that, will you? Then see if you can fish out the card with little Shirley McGlone's name on it. If it's kept out it'll remind me to fill it in afterwards.' She drummed her fingers on the steering wheel. 'Paperwork's a pain. Still, the triple duties of nursing, midwifery and health visiting do give variety even if Bell here gives me a run for my money.'

She stopped the car outside the house with the smoking chimney, got out and stretched her back. She nodded at the garden which was full of rusting vehicles. 'You'll see our family's taken their old home with them. It seems it's taking them longer to settle in the house than the garden. Anyway, let's catch them before they pretend they're not at home. Come on.'

She pushed on the garden gate. 'Blast!'

The garden gate gave a warning creak. A small anxious face peered round a tattered net curtain and disappeared so quickly I wondered if I had imagined it. Then I heard a door slam.

'Who's she?' A voice came through the letterbox.

Sister Shiach bent down and spoke through it as if talking into a telephone receiver. 'It's okay, Bell. She's new. I'm training her.' She spoke in a wheedling way. 'Come on now. Open the door. I'm so proud of the way you're settling in. I've been telling her about you and know she'd like to meet you.'

A tall girl with jet-black hair inched the door open. She said, 'Spy on me, more like. Don't you be giving me that stupid sweet talk.' Despite the sour tone, she opened the door wider.

She wore wellingtons, which as she grudgingly stepped back to allow us in left muddy tracks on the linoleum in the hallway. Her cardigan, worn over a washed-out pinafore apron, was full of holes and a dismal grey. Still, it couldn't dim the sparkle of her brown eyes and her gold earrings. They danced as she shook her head. 'It's no worth you coming further, the wee one's out playing.'

'No, I'm not, Mam. I'm here.'

The small child whose face I'd seen at the window came and stood beside us. 'I camed round from the back door,' she offered. She, too, was wearing wellies, but on the wrong feet, and a coat that even though someone had hacked a bit off, still trailed on the ground. She sneaked behind her mother, who put a protective hand round her shoulder. 'It's all right, Shirl. It's only the nurse and,' she viewed me with narrowed eyes, 'some other woman, and I suppose you'd better come on ben.' In a combative way she added, 'We're not tidy.'

'You're fine. We came to see you, not the house,' said Sister Shiach.

We went into the living room where she steered a safe course past piles of *Exchange and Mart* magazines to car seats cosily arranged by a fire sulking in the grate. Covering it, more or less, was a battered-looking fireguard. To Bell's evident surprise, her visitor admired it.

'It's grand you've got that,' she said, nodding towards Shirley. 'You wouldn't want the wee one tripping and having an accident, would you?'

'Course not,' her mother sounded outraged. 'I know how to look after my bairns.'

'And the others'll be at school?' enquired Sister Shiach, looking into the flames.

'Course.' Bell's voice carried less conviction.

'It can't be easy settling down to a school routine. Up till now, you've all led a life of freedom.' Sister Shiach was sympathetic. 'But if they do nothing else at school other than learn to read, it'll have been worthwhile.'

'Aye. I suppose.'

There was half a loaf of white Sliced Pan on a table alongside a tin of syrup with a knife sticking out of it. I put the bag of clothes out of its sticky range but near enough for Shirley to see. Becoming bolder at the lack of attention, she moved toward it. She'd the rosy cheeks of an outdoor person. Perhaps that's why the coat particularly fascinated her, or maybe it was its toggles. Her small grubby fingers inched towards, then started to play with them.

'That's right bonny,' she said, managing a hop of excitement despite the wellies and trailing coat. A gathering of snot collected under her snub nose.

'Here,' Bell said, taking a corner of her apron to wipe it away, 'I hope that's not all for us. We don't take charity, you know.' Her eyes flashed and she folded her arms.

A large tear rolled down Shirley's cheek. 'Aw, Mam! I've see-ed a bonny coat. It's like hers next door has.'

'And she's a spoilt wee brat.' Sister Shiach, eyes twinkling, opened her mouth wide then shut it. But Bell ignored the hint for tact and continued, 'Her mother's a snobby cow. Says us tinks comin' here's lowering the tone o' the place.'

She seized the bag and coat and thrust them at me. 'Here! You take these. Just seeing fancy clothes would fill any bairn's head with nonsense. They're no for the like of us.'

Whilst Shirley gave herself up to soundless sobbing, Bell's jaw hardened. She's not going to back down, I thought.

31

6

ON THE ROAD

'And what makes you think you're getting these for nothing?' Sister Shiach sounded surprised. Sighing in exasperation, she pointed at a rag-rug in front of the fire. The last time I'd seen one was a generation ago, made by my thrifty grandmother from the remnants of old clothes. 'Look, Bell, you're good at making these. I could use one for Jomo in the car.'

'Yon wee mongrel? You're wanting a rug for your dog!' Bell gave a disbelieving cry. 'Next thing you'll be telling me to knit him a waistcoat!'

'He's purebred, and don't you let him hear you say otherwise.' Sister Shiach wagged a finger and continued, 'And no, his own coat does him fine. But a rug would help to keep my car clean. Sometimes I've to bath the wee blighter before he gets near it.' She sighed and clapped her hands to her side. 'Dogs!'

Despite herself, Bell couldn't help laughing. 'D'you hear that, Shirl? Nurse here baths her dog. She should try it on bairns instead.'

But Shirley was too engrossed sniffing and poking her fingers into the bag to answer.

'It's bad enough doing my lot!' Bell went on, 'I've enough of a problem getting them near a tap.'

'You tell them about Jomo then. Say he actually likes the water

32

and it certainly stops him scratching.' There was a small pause, then Sister Shiach whispered, 'Nobody likes an itch, do they?'

'Oh, Mameeee! Can we no keep these?' Shirley pleaded.

Bell shrugged. 'Oh well, if it pleases you, I suppose so, though I'm no sure when I'll find the time to make another rug.'

Shirley hauled off her old coat and put on the duffle. Even though it wasn't a perfect fit it was certainly an improvement on the old one. As she pulled up the hood, her little face sent out a sunbeam that, despite herself, Bell returned.

'Here!' She went to help with the toggle buttons, but Shirley had already fastened them.

'I see she's got your clever fingers,' said Sister Shiach. 'She'll be the one to help you make that rug and, look, you can use her old coat for material now. It's the same colour as Jomo.' She laughed. 'He'll think it's his mother!'

The coat had given Shirley enough confidence to approach her benefactress. 'Can I see your wee doggy?'

'Of course – if you change your wellies to the right feet. I don't want you falling in the mud and spoiling your bonny new coat. Look, put back your hood for a minute so you can see what you're doing.'

I caught Sister Shiach giving a quick glance at Shirley's mop head as she bent over her boots. Then, taking her small hand in hers, she said, 'Are you readeeee? Jomo loves a visitor.'

Bell, arms akimbo, watched us from her door. She'd have seen the big welcome the dog gave Shirley. On the other hand, she might not have noticed the bottles of orange juice and shampoo handed to her daughter, nor given it much thought when Shirley, in turn and with her feet properly aligned, went skipping back to the house and gave them to her.

'Sometimes, and this is an awful thing to say, it's an advantage that some of our patients can't read,' Sister Shiach mused. 'With a bit of luck, Bell won't know that that shampoo's for hair infestation. Come on, let's go in case she does and throws a brick at us.' As she started the car, she said, 'I wish the next visit was as easy.'

It had begun to snow. The one wiper worked hard to clear the windscreen but the flakes sliding down the glass were huge. Outwith the wiper's sweep, they collected in small drifts, gradually confining our vision to a sort of tunnel view.

Maybe that's why we didn't see the cat running across the road until the last minute. Sister Shiach touched the brakes and the car skidded. Jomo sat up and whined, but whether it was through fright or because he'd seen the animal and been unable to chase it wasn't clear. Still, he put himself back into sentry position, his small body quivering with tension.

As we resumed our progress, Sister Shiach patted the dog in a reassuring way. Peering out from under a meantime surplus but pulled-down sun visor, she said, 'I think you should maybe head home to Conon Bridge and, whilst on your way, could you pop in and check on the Duthie boys? You know, the ones we visited a few days ago. Sometimes they're not very clever about keeping warm and Willie's iron injections mightn't have started to kick in yet. He'll still be vulnerable to the cold.' She seemed completely unfazed by the increasing whiteout and the fact that the car's indicator remained in the turn-right position.

As for me, I was beginning to feel squeamish. Travel sickness, that legacy from childhood, still bothered me. Getting out of the car would, I knew, be a help, still I felt I had to ask, 'You were saying you'd a difficult patient. Won't you need a hand?'

Casually holding the steering wheel as the car momentarily mounted the pavement, my mentor was matter-of-fact. 'No. What I meant was my patient's *life* was difficult. You see, she's actually living in a tent and with her bairn.'

Despite the companionable fug in the car, I shivered and instinctively rubbed my arms. 'A tent? You're joking!'

'I wish I was.'

The car went into another skid. Jomo whimpered and I held back a scream. With no other traffic on the road, the single wiper labouring and snow covering the other windows, the inside of the car was dark and like a little world on its own. If we got stuck or lost, I wondered who'd know. Who'd be daft enough to be out in weather like this?

'I've a shovel and rug in the boot,' Sister Shiach said, as if reading my thoughts, 'but the weather forecast said it should be clear by early evening. Och, we'll be all right.' She put the pedal down hard. 'But I'll need to get on if I want to see her today.'

'Why's she where she is?' I wondered.

'She's fallen out with her family and is now staying in a bell tent. It's just on the outskirts of town.'

'But she'll be frozen! Is there a man around?'

Sister Shiach was matter-of-fact again. 'I'm not sure. I don't ask. I think he's probably like Bell's husband. Comes and goes. But my tent lady's a wee coper and she's near a wood so she's plenty fuel. Believe it or not, there's a wood-burning stove in that tent.' She blew out her cheeks in a monumental sigh. 'In weather like this, I don't know whether to think that's a good or a bad thing. Not so long ago, her daughter fell against that stove. It's taken ages for her burns to heal.'

She rubbed her forehead in despair. 'She'd have grown into a beautiful woman if half of her face hadn't been completely disfigured. It's a tragedy. Now I just need to check they're at least alive. The mother's torn apart with guilt and I bet she's not been eating either. I'll nip to my house and get her some soup just in case, and when we're there you can pick up your car.'

* * *

Like the sign announcing that we were at the home of the District Nursing Sister, my car also wore a mantle of snow. It was a Morris Minor as well. It seemed that the county council had chosen our cars to match our uniforms. In Sister Shiach's view, no discriminating motorist could possibly have chosen such a dismal blue. Still, in this weather, my white Imp would be hard to see so, glad of any distinguishing colour, I cleared the snow off the Morris's bonnet.

Sister Shiach banged on it in a hearty fashion. 'That's fine. Now we'll easily find you if you land in a drift and you don't appear tomorrow. Drive slowly and you'll be fine. Look, it's even stopped snowing. Good luck with the Duthies and I'll see you tomorrow morning after you do that home visit to the captain. Just remember, when you're bathing him he can get a bit fruity.' Her eyes brimmed with mischief then, calling into her car to tell Jomo she'd be back in a minute, she turned towards the house.

I knew where the Duthies lived. I'd met them on my first day, which coincided with the last one of Willie's iron-injection course treating his anaemia.

Jock, his brother, had been a roadman. He'd worked in different parts of Ross-shire, but latterly worked singly on the one on which his house stood. Had it received the same meticulous attention it would not now have ferns that were growing out of its drain ipes or a door which was short of a latch.

On our way there, Sister Shiach had explained, 'Jock and Willie are old bachelors. Now, Willie's the shy one. Actually, if he was ever at school they might have called him slow, but he's no daft.'

She shook her head then continued, 'I've had to use all my powers of persuasion to let me give him those iron injections, especially as they need to go into his hip. It was only when I told him he hadn't enough flesh on his arm to soak up the iron he allowed me enough space for the needle to go in. Thank goodness he did. I didn't fancy grappling with him to get his long johns off.'

36

I'd noticed them dancing on the washing line a week later, on my way to work. 'Well, at least the boys have taken your advice about washing them,' I'd said, then gradually grew more concerned seeing them still there a couple of days after that.

'It's probably Willie's idea of laundering,' Sister Shiach said. 'He's the housekeeper and even though Jock's retired, that's still the case.' She cast her eyes heavenward. 'It wouldn't occur to Jock to take them in. I'm not even sure if Willie would have washed them. He'll probably think the stuff falling from Heaven will do as good a laundry job as him.'

Observation had been one of the key skills our nursing tutors had gone on and on about when we were training. They hadn't mentioned clothes on washing lines but in this case they could prove to be a barometer for health. It could be just laziness but the length of time Willie's long johns were hanging outside might be a matter of concern.

I drove out of Dingwall at a crawling pace, getting more confident as the winter tread-tyres bit on the road surface. I gradually picked up speed, hoping to reach the brothers before dark, but then suddenly I let my foot slip off the accelerator. When I put it back down, I was too heavy with it. The car roared and jerked forward. Not a good time to hit ice.

As if bent on its own destination, the car glided out of control. Braking, I was quick to learn, made it worse. Now facing in the wrong direction, perilously close to a ditch and in a gathering gloom, I prayed for a return of nerve, a lighter foot and a biddable car. A traffic-free road would be an added blessing.

At least I was lucky in that respect. The road stayed empty as, slowly and fearfully, I managed to get the car back on course. As for nerve, anxiety made me grip the steering wheel so hard I'd to practically unlock my hands from it when at last I arrived at the brothers' house.

It was just before dark and the long johns were still on the line. Freeze-framed, they looked as if to be worn they'd need to be jumped into.

On that first visit, hens had been scratching in a netted-off area, complete with a snug-looking little house Jock said he'd made for them. Now they were, sensibly, inside it. I could hear them clucking and imagined they'd be a lot warmer under their felt roof than the Duthies with their corrugated iron one.

I knew Jock was kind to animals. I remembered him talking fondly about them whilst Willie was getting his injection. He'd said, 'When I was working I'd see lots of injured beasties and I'd take them home on this.' He banged on the saddle of a classy-looking Raleigh propped inside the house's lobby. 'Then I'd try to mend them, mend them.'

Remembering our conversation, I knocked on the door, and fearful I might stand on some ill animal, stepped with care inside.

Jock met me with a pleased, 'It's the wee nursie. Come away. Come away!' He had a habit of repeating the last words twice, then whistling to fill any conversational gaps. Maybe with him latterly working on his own it made him want to communicate for a bit of company, even if it was just with himself. Or maybe he was compensating for Willie. Not a man for either long speeches or much eye contact, he did manage a few 'ayes,' and lots of 'uh-huhs'. The one word he did seem to enjoy saying was 'cheerio'.

Now I asked where he was, wondering if he'd fled at the sound of my voice.

'He's in bed, in bed, yes-yes,' Jock nodded at a sagging chair beside the unlit fire. 'He feels the cold, terrible, yes, terrible.' Jock's outdoor life having clearly inured him to a sub-zero temperature must have made him immune to an atmosphere where you could see your breath.

I was sure Willie would be horrified, but I persevered. 'Would he mind if I said hello to him?'

'He's asleep, asleep.' Jock took off his woolly cap, scratched his bald head then, replacing it, continued, 'Jee whiz – what a man to sleep, to sleep.' He nodded at an ornate clock on the mantelpiece. Presented to Jock on his retirement, it had *Tempus Fugit* inscribed on it. As if flying-time didn't apply to his brother, he declared, 'He's been like that for ages, ages!'

'I'll not disturb him, but maybe I'll have a wee peek.' I headed for a room adjoining the living room. 'Where's the light?'

'Wait you! Wait you!' Jock stepped before me and with infinite care switched it on. It flickered into a dismal light provided by a naked bulb. I shivered as the room temperature stopped me in my tracks. It was even colder than in the living room. A set of orange false teeth grinned up at me from the floor just as I saw a shape in the bed. It was under some flimsy-looking bedclothes and lay as still as the grave.

7

COLD COMFORT

There's one thing about an emergency. It removes the insignificant. My chilled feet were nothing compared to the cold lumps sticking out from the bottom of the bed. I quickly established that the cold extended to the rest of Willie's body. His face was pale as a ghost, his skin had the clammy feel of a corpse, and he was only wearing a vest. I didn't need a thermometer to diagnose hypothermia. Willie's condition was serious but at least I could tell on taking his pulse and feeling its sluggish flicker that he was still alive.

I prodded him gently, unsurprised when nothing happened. Knowing Willie's reluctance to speak, I didn't expect floods of eloquence. Still, it'd have been lovely to have heard a grunt.

'See what a grand sleeper he is, he is.' Jock stood in the doorway and spoke in admiration.

I ran over to him, grabbed his hat and stuck it on Willie's head. 'Look, Jock, if he was any colder, he'd be frozen stiff. That's a fine enough vest he's got on but have you any scarves, more blankets and have you a phone?'

Jock patted his head as if to check his hat had really gone. 'Yes-yes and no. What would we be doing with a telyphone? A telyphone?' He looked at me in astonishment.

'Making a 999 call,' I could've said, only I didn't want to alarm a perfectly healthy man whose rosy complexion had just faded to a worrying grey. One patient was enough.

I glanced through a grimy window across which a tattered lace curtain was stretched. The night was far darker now but the sky had cleared, leaving some deeply red-tinged clouds, suggesting that tomorrow might bring more settled weather. Standing close to the house was a tree. It was leafless, showing still and black against the skyline, whilst the fallen snow made everywhere else sparkle. It could have been a magical scene had there not been someone so completely lost to it.

In hospital, doctors were around to take ultimate responsibility. I hadn't anticipated this level of drama on district but now, after such a short time, I was in the thick of it. Willie's life depended on me taking the right action.

'Always remember us girls are guests in people's houses and sometimes not very welcome ones at that,' Sister Shiach had advised, 'so it's important you don't act as if you owned the place.'

I considered this for half a second, then in a steely mode that would have appealed far more to Sister Gall, I drilled out the words, 'Look here, Jock. We've got to get Willie's temperature back up. He's ill, you know. We must get that fire on and you'll need to find more bedclothes. Quickly now!' Then belatedly, 'Please.'

But Jock had lost the place thanks either to my tone or to being deprived of his hat. Lost to despair, he just clutched his egg-like head and softly moaned. At length he managed, 'Oh, Nursie, Nursie, my brother!' He hadn't even repeated himself. He was ashen-faced. This could be serious. So much for people taking instruction.

Personal accountability was one of the reasons I wanted to be a district nurse. In hospital, I hadn't cared for leading a team, hadn't felt I would need to have the same instructional expertise on district. Now here I was, with a team of just one whom I'd managed to put in as much in danger of collapse as my existing patient.

My call then. Given the domestic circumstances, I'd have to settle for something unconventional.

I took Jock's arm and steered him towards the bed, grateful it was a three-quarter size. 'Okay, Jock, I know you'll think this is daft, but if you want to be really, really helpful, climb in with Willie then hold onto him for dear life.'

My team member stepped back, looking horrified. 'What! He's my brother, he'll no like that.'

'Well, that might be a good thing. Anything to make his brain register. In the meantime, your body heat will transfer to him. In fact, you could just be his lifesaver. Go on!'

Somewhere in my training, after all, I must've picked up on how to give a command that gave a result because Jock threw himself on the bed. As he climbed under the bedclothes, there was a clunk as he kicked off his boots and they hit the floor. A minute later, as if steeling himself, he rolled Willie on his side, and put his arm round him.

'That's great. Cuddle up close and keep your arm there. It'll stop him rolling out. Now, either whistle or chat to him, whilst I get some more bedclothes.'

Jock's whistle was a tuneless accompaniment as I rushed through to his bedroom. I grabbed an ancient purple quilt and grey blankets off the bed and seized a pair of socks so grimy they must have been used instead of shoes.

'That's my socks, and my quilt, my quilt!' protested Jock as I returned, laden. 'And, Nursie, I'm no complainin' but you'll have me boiling, boiling!' And certainly his face had returned to its usual rosy hue. Still, after I'd navigated the socks past Willie's long, horny toenails and onto his feet, I thought it best to take both of the brothers' pulses.

'You're fine,' I said to Jock, wishing my real patient was registering the same healthy beat. 'And I'll make sure you get the socks back. Anyway, you're doing a grand job. You're better than a hot water bottle.'

'As long as I don't start leaking, leaking.' Even if beads of sweat were forming on Jock's brow, he was beginning to relax and able to tell me where I could get the necessary to start the fire.

'Look in the range cupboard. Plenty kindlers there,' he said. 'And you'll get paper under Willie's chair-cushion, cushion. That's where he keeps the *P&J*.'

Willie was never going to get a medal for housekeeping but the sticks piled inside the wee range were stacked with such precision it seemed a shame to use them. There was a bonus to the unusual use of the oven too, for the sticks were bone dry. Soon I'd a good fire going.

Casting flickering shapes on the walls, it brought a little cheer to the sparsely furnished room and ill-lit living room. Lampshades wouldn't have had a high rating on the brothers' shopping list but at least the house had electricity so that a hot drink would be possible. The thought was encouraging, but I'd been so engrossed on tending the fire I hadn't noticed that Jock had stopped whistling.

I rushed through to the bedroom. To my surprised relief, he'd actually fallen asleep. With his pink scalp and his wrinkles relaxed in slumber he looked like an elderly untroubled cherub. I breathed again, then checked Willie. He was beginning to get back some colour, and his pulse and temperature were picking up.

I knew there was a farmhouse just along the road. Maybe they had a phone. It was worth a try.

'I'm going to ask your neighbours for a bit of help,' I whispered to the two recumbent forms, 'and I'll be right back.'

Although the distance between the houses was short, I was glad to get there without the Morris slipping off the farm road.

'Mercy me!' exclaimed the lady who answered the door to my frantic knock. She shouted to someone over her shoulder, 'Hugh, come here! There's a car with a nurse here and she's saying the boys are in big trouble.'

Confidentiality wasn't a big issue, I thought, forgiving myself for my garbled introduction. 'Actually, if I could use your phone that would be a great help.' I said, then, trying for a less dramatic approach, 'I'm sure they're going to be fine but I'd just like to speak to Sister Shiach first.'

'Ah! Sister Shiach! She's one girl. She'll know what to do. Did she not deliver all our children, Hugh?' With the inference that my mentor couldn't have had a better qualification or the world to be in better hands, the woman relaxed and leant against the door jamb. As if to illustrate her point, two sturdy-looking youngsters joined her and beamed up at me. They had a well-fed look and confident way that I would have loved Bell's Shirl to have had.

Meanwhile, Hugh, perhaps more attuned to anxiety, came to the door and beckoned me in, saying to his wife, 'Och, stop your blethering. Can't you see the lassie needs the phone? Once she's spoken to Sister then we'll help as best we can. Come on, Nurse, it's in the kitchen, and so are we. Oh, sorry, Hugh Campbell,' he added, sticking out his hand.

He didn't say, but it was obvious from the half-empty plates that they were in the middle of their tea. The lingering smell of bacon made me feel hungry and my fingers tingled, registering that frostbite had moved from probable to less likely. The family made light of my apologies for interrupting, showed me the phone then sat down to listen with friendly interest.

Sister Shiach answered the phone on the first ring. Once I'd finished, she was matter-of-fact. 'Well it's good that his temp's going up. You've done fine, but it sounds as if he'd be the better of a right thaw-out so he's probably best in hospital. He won't want to go, of course but he's in no position to object. Once he is there, he'll get a good chance to be built up as well. I'll call the doctor, tell him Willie needs to be admitted to the Ross Memorial.'

'Yes, it's great that Dingwall's got a hospital.'

'Uh-huh, and you'll need to go with him in the ambulance you're about to call. Once you've done that, get back to the boys. Stay with them and keep warm yourself. Their neighbours are good folk, really helpful. They're always fretting about the Duthies so if they want to help, you could ask them if they've any spare soup. Jock could probably do with some.' She added, 'I expect the boys have plenty firewood. They must. From time to time, they give some to the Campbells. I'll let you get on to make that ambulance call now but,' she dropped her voice, 'you'll already know you've got a bit of an emergency on your hands.'

I'd never dialled 999 before and the watching family was plainly impressed when I did.

'Thanks for that,' I said, replacing the receiver, 'but now I have to get back. They say they're on their way.'

'Right, I'll come with you to make sure you manage on the road,' said Hugh, grabbing a huge overcoat. 'I'll go and start the Land Rover.'

Mrs Campbell, who must have heard the phone conversation, put in, 'And I'll give you some soup. It's lucky you called when you did. We had some for tea. It's lentil. I know the boys like that. Sometimes they'll accept something, but only if we take some of their sticks. They're far too proud for their own good. Look!' She brandished a thermos. 'I'll fill this and there'll be some for you too. You must be perishing. The Duthies' house is like an ice block. We do worry about them. It's good to get this chance to really help them.'

I nearly told her not to hurry. The warm kitchen with its

comfortable furnishings and kindly folk made the idea of returning to an igloo an even chillier prospect than it already was.

I said, 'I'm torn between worrying that I've left the Duthies with such a big blaze, it's put the house on fire or,' I leant against the Rayburn cooker's rail, 'it's gone out. In which case, I'll be glad of this warm up.'

Mrs Campbell was bustling about with the briskness of a woman on a mission. She was reassuring. 'We'd have seen the flames if it had. Anyway, Hugh will go with you, make sure you get back quickly and safely. The farm road can be tricky. Well done for getting here in one bit. You could easily have landed in a ditch.' Handing over the thermos she said, 'See you, and have some of that now and I'd advise using the cap. You might not survive eating from a Duthie plate.'

I was moved by her kindness. What with herself and her husband so enthusiastically helping, I went out into the night feeling that, from one minute of being on my own, I'd now got a committed team on side. Added to that was the Campbells' Land Rover. With its throaty roar bellowing into the night, the engine was a reassuringly powerful sound.

Hugh had brought it to the house and, opening the door, shouted above the racket, 'I'll go first and you follow my tracks. But mind how you go. I don't want to have to pull you out. Not with the Duthies needing us so urgently.' He had the easy manner of someone who'd consider this an insignificant but unnecessary interruption.

Diligently, I maintained a steady course behind him, trying not to be hypnotised by our car lights. Their beams occasionally streaming up into the sky were like spotlights, merging and crossing as if in some strange angular dance. I had to remind myself that they weren't giving a display, merely highlighting the road's hidden bumps.

The Morris Minor, instead of behaving like a skittish colt, became strangely biddable. You'd never have thought the wretch ever had an independent thought. I'd have a word with her when we got home. She was lucky my boots were too flimsy to give her a sharp kick.

For now, however, we'd arrived at the Duthie house. At least it hadn't gone on fire. It was a relief too when Jock came to meet us. Giving Hugh a cursory nod, he said in a complaining sort of way, 'I couldna sleep. Willie's got awful restless. He never did like sharing a bed.' He patted an old beret, last seen covering the bicycle seat and now on his head. 'And he's saying awful daft things, daft things.'

'Well, you'll be glad to hear that's good news,' I said heartily. 'It means he's coming back to us. We've organised an ambulance to take him to hospital just to make sure he gets on the mend as quickly as possible.'

'He won't like that, like that, but it's maybe for the best.' Jock wiped his brow and shook his head. 'Forbye that I'd like to sleep in my own bed too, too.'

A siren wailed in the distance.

'That's Willie's taxi,' said Hugh, who was either stamping his feet clear of snow or avoiding frostbite. 'And I know at least one person who'll be pleased to see it, eh, Nurse?'

8

TAKING THE PLUNGE

The long johns were beginning to take on a personality. They were now on my own washing line and dancing in the wind as if to a jig. I'd taken them home after my trip to the hospital with Willie.

Getting him ready, I'd presumed his underwear was limited to the one garment meantime freezing on the Duthie washing line. Jock was stressed enough without me asking for pyjamas so I'd grabbed an old jacket off a peg on the back of the bedroom door and used it to cover Willie as best I could.

The Ross Memorial Hospital ran with such a smooth and kind efficiency, the staff seemed unsurprised at a patient arriving and wearing something more suitable for his top half than the bottom. They changed him into more conventional wear. When I got back to Jock I told him that Willie was in safe hands, rapidly thawing and very smart in striped flannelette pyjamas.

He scratched his brow and said, 'He wisna very respectable when he left here. He'll no be right till he gets these back on, back on.' He'd nodded at the long johns now draped over Willie's chair and steaming gently. There was a worrying human smell coming from them.

I'd suggested I could take them home. 'They could probably do with a wee rinse,' I said, and thought Willie might get a surprise when he recovered consciousness. He was such a private, shy man

I hoped that dressed in brightly coloured pyjamas might not be as big a shock to his system as waking up in a hospital bed.

As Jock chewed over my offer, I continued, 'We're lucky, you know. The nurses' houses are so well equipped we've even got washing machines.' Looking round the Duthie's ill-furnished house, I thought guiltily about my own little cottage. I was sure Miss Macleod had had a hand in its well-appointed, carpeted and snug comfort.

As soon as I said I was going home, Jock looked pleased. He rubbed his hands and nodded his head. 'Yes! That's best. With my brother out of the house and your car outside late, we wouldn't want people to start speaking, speaking.'

Last night's red sky had been an accurate sign that better weather was on its way. In the morning, with the wind promising a drying day and shifting the snow into piebald patches, I'd pinned out the long johns before heading for work.

Driving towards Dingwall, I thought about Captain Saunders-Hewitt's alleged fruitiness. In my hospital experience, I'd found a slight slap with a wet facecloth usually cured the ailment. I just hoped he didn't use a sponge. That would be hopeless.

The Saunders-Hewitts lived in a quiet cul-de-sac very different from Bell's street. Their house, standing in huge grounds taken over by rhododendrons, may have had a more glorious past, but it still looked imposing.

'A local lady goes in every day to help but the Captain's a bit of a lad. Thinks he's above personal hygiene,' Sister Shiach had explained. 'Both the Saunders-Hewitts are getting a bit frail now and if we didn't go in, his wife might give up on him – and maybe herself as well. Personally, I think they could manage fine with a little encouragement. And they have their little indulgences.' She mimed someone emptying a glass. 'I'm never sure what to expect

49

from a visit but don't you take any nonsense from him. Stick him in the bath and make sure he scrubs his back. *Himself.*

There was no reply when I hammered on the big brass doorknocker but the creak as I opened the door would have wakened the dead. Yet still there was no answer. I listened hard. There was the occasional creak and groan of an old house in failing health but if there were any ghosts, I figured that they should be of animals killed for sport. Trophies of them were everywhere.

Then I heard a giggle. It came from upstairs.

'Hello?' I called from the huge hallway. My footsteps echoing on the wooden floor were suddenly muffled by a tiger skin. A stopped grandfather clock said it was midnight.

'Ooops! Sorry,' I said, suddenly aware of being watched. But it was only the glazed eyes of a stag, its head mounted on the wall at the top of the stairs, the carpet of which was threadbare. More care had been lavished on the brass rods securing it. I suspected the Saunders-Hewitts hadn't been responsible for their bright gleam, but probably were the source of noises coming from above.

As I climbed the stairs, I held my nursing bag before me, trusting that both it and my uniform would identify me as their nurse. As I went I interspersed my helloes with discreet coughs. I could hear the sounds were coming from a room at the end of a wood-panelled corridor.

It was in darkness. Maybe I'd the wrong room but before I went to turn back, a bedside light was switched on.

'Oh! Look what we've got, Charles. It's a dear little nurse!' The light shone on a large stone on a thin finger of an elderly lady who had the sleek elegance of a greyhound. She was still in bed along with, I presumed and rather hoped, my patient. She must have liked jewellery because she also wore pearls. He favoured a cravat and as far as I could see without actually staring, not much else.

He said, 'By Jove, it is. Ha! We shought you might be a burglar. But come in, do, do!' He nudged his partner. 'We inshist, don't we, Ginny?'

'Rather!' Ginny was enthusiastic.

An empty sherry bottle lay on the floor. It might explain Charles's ruddy complexion, the couple's cheery way and a few other things I didn't care to explore.

Aiming my gaze at an oil painting of a stag in better health than the one on the staircase, I said, 'Oooh, sorry. Look! I'll come back in an hour.'

Ginny shot up. She wasn't wearing anything either. 'No, my dear! You mustn't. We'll get a frightful row from Sister Shiach if she hears we've been messing up your routine. It's just we weren't expecting you so soon. She did tell us you'd be coming but she didn't say you'd be so young.' Now, she didn't sound so pleased but continued, 'Only we didn't know when.'

Charles rubbed his hands and tidied his moustache over large yellow teeth. If it hadn't been for the sherry bottle I might have thought he'd had a stroke as he slurred, 'She didn't shay to expeck a young filly though, did she?' His eyes gleamed.

I'd a quick think. Whatever hazard he might present, naked or otherwise, I needed to get him sober. I moved to the curtains and jerked them open. The little metal wheels securing them to a rail screamed.

'I shay!' Charles put his hands over his ears whilst Ginny fumbled in the bedclothes. 'Where's those dratted gaspers?' She had the wheeze of an enthusiastic smoker. 'Charles darling, have you got the lighter?'

One minute I'm trying to get a patient warm in bed and the next I'm trying to stop one going on fire, I thought, deciding on a brisk approach.

'I'm a great believer in the restorative power of fresh air,' I declared, and shot up the window. A chilly draught accompanied my words. 'Now, I'm going to pop downstairs, make you something to drink and once you've had that, you'll be ready for your bath, Captain.'

'Brrh! Ginny, put down your chiggy and warm me up.' My patient had burrowed down under the bedclothes, leaving just his eyes and moustache visible. The bedclothes started to move as if alive.

Ginny slapped at them, inhaling as deeply as someone gasping for air. 'Ooh, you naughty boy!' Casually, she put her cigarette to the side.

If it hadn't been for the fire risk I might just have left them to it, said I'd call another day. Instead I made a big show of shoving the window up another couple of inches then, promising a swift return, hurried downstairs.

I left the kitchen door open and made the kettle whistle several times, hoping it would have alerted the Saunders-Hewitts to progress. When I carried two cups of strong Camp Coffee back upstairs, Charles was sitting up and now wearing silk pyjamas so grand they could do for a state occasion.

'What a dishturber of the peashe you are,' he complained. 'Jusht when Ginny and I were shettling down again, I'd to get up and dreshed to shut that damn window.' He looked at the coffee. 'And I don't want thish. I shuspect it tashtes vile.'

'I'd be happier if you did drink it,' I said, pleased at the bad temper. He must be sobering up. 'Sister Shiach said you liked something strong to start you for the day. I'm presuming she meant coffee. I have to meet her quite soon.' I made a big play of consulting my watch. 'We're running a bit out of time, I'd hate to have to tell her you've missed out on your bath.'

Ginny plucked his arm. 'Just do as the wee nursie says. We mustn't upset Sister Shiach.' She gave a genteel hiccup, smoothed back her grey hair and placed a finger over her lips. 'Oooh, excuse me.' The red nail varnish showed vivid against her pale face.

Leaving the Captain unhappily slurping, I looked for the bathroom and found a huge room with an enormous bath in the middle of it. Some worrying plumbing noises came from a towel rail with bars the size of organ pipes. But at least it was warming the large monogrammed towel laid over it and took the chill from the high-ceilinged room.

'Always run cold water first in any bath. You don't want to scald your patient.' Remembering a past nursing tutor's advice, I turned on the tap. Water gushed from it as if it came from the Falls of Glomach and was so noisy I didn't hear my patient arriving.

'No!' I cried, but too late. He'd thrown away his pyjamas, and before I could stop him, he'd plunged into a bath half-full of freezing water.

9

MEN MAY WORK

Jomo wagged his tail and cocked his head as he watched his mistress leaning helplessly over her desk. Wiping away tears of laughter, she asked, 'So what happened after the Captain took to the water?'

We were in a small room in her house. I expect it was meant for office work and storing nursing equipment, but it was more like a drapery store. A hand towel fell from a variety of sheets and clothes cramming the surrounding shelves. I picked it up, and trying to find a space to shove it back, said, 'I learnt two things about the Captain this morning. One, he can easily and quickly get out of a bath and two, a cold one's a great way to sober him up. Mind you, with all his squeals and protests you'd have thought his wife would have lain low, but she came through to investigate.' I mimed a pistol to my head. 'She insisted she fill the bath instead of me doing it and she'd help him get back in. It was completely obvious to her that I wasn't competent enough.'

I didn't add that Ginny had also said she was protecting her husband against flighty pieces, a remark which had thoroughly interested the Captain and thoroughly annoyed me.

The remark might still have rankled had Sister Shiach not seemed so pleased. Clapping her hands twice, she said, 'Well, that's just fine. And there was me feeling sorry for her! She can get on with helping him. It'll save me the hassle of visiting. There's lots more people needing my time than the bloomin' Saunders-Hewitts. I've only really been going there to support her, but it sounds like she's managing fine, if in her own way.'

'Well, to tell you the truth,' I said, 'I think she quite enjoyed the experience. She must have. She actually threw off her kimono, pulled off her necklaces, shouted, "Look! Charles, I'm casting my pearls before swine," then she dived in. There was a bit of a splash,' I reflected. 'You're lucky to see me. For a minute I thought I'd be washed away in a tidal wave. Anyway, I got out before I could see any more creative uses of a loofah.'

Chuckling, Sister Shiach opened a green book with a list of names and columns beside them. She took a red pen and put a tick beside the Captain's name. 'To show he's had a visit,' she explained, then she stroked a line through it. 'There! I'll give him a follow-up call, tell him he's off the books and I'm so pleased he's able to bathe himself but to keep an eye on his wife when she's there too. It'd be good for him to take some responsibility for *her* for a change.'

Had Jomo had a watch, he'd have been checking it. As it was, he was studying the door with fixed interest then running to his mistress and pawing at her boots. I wished I had boots like hers. They looked far more useful than my trendy numbers, which leaked and seemed to embrace the cold. My toes were sore when they weren't itching. Maybe I was getting chilblains. Sensible boots would probably solve the problem. Thinking about the bell-tent lady and how exposed to cold she must be made me feel lucky I'd such a simple solution.

Sister Shiach shrugged into her coat. 'Okay, Jomo, we'll go. Come on, troops.'

As I got into her car I said, 'I didn't get round to asking you last night, but were the bell-tenters all right?'

She shook her head. 'Not really. It was so cold I was anxious about them. It was a good thing I took them soup and the mum wasn't too proud to take it. The stove was going great guns so I thought that as long as they didn't put their tent on fire they'd survive.' She wiped the windscreen with the back of her gloved hand and peered up at the sky. 'Thank God the weather's better today. Still, I think Mum's beginning to realise she can't go it alone. I'm going to have a word with her doctor today. See if we can get her a house. I bet there'll be one near Bell shortly.'

Drumming her fingers on the steering wheel, she continued, 'From the way she spoke yesterday, her present neighbour'll soon be wanting a shift. She's not going to stay at the end of Bell's tongue for long. What d'you say, Jomo?' Thoughtfully, she stroked his head.

Jomo stood up to wag his tail, which made Sister Shiach nod her head. 'Yes, I think so too. And if that house does become available, I'm sure if I asked Bell to help the bell-tenters settle in, she'd do it gladly. She knows what such a lifestyle change that is. Then, the wee one's much the same age as Shirley – they'd be company for each other and that'd be good for their confidence, especially when they start school. It's not good for anybody to shut themselves away.'

She started the car then, as if readying for take-off, revved the engine. Above its roar she shouted, 'The couple we're going to visit may have different home circumstances from my bell-tenters but they're not so different when it comes to hiding away.' She crashed the car into gear, pushing me back in my seat, then continued in a softer voice, 'Now I know you're anxious about seeing folk in a health visitor capacity. This visit'll maybe give you a chance to see that using your common sense can work fine even if you haven't got a certificate.' She tapped her head. 'Using this is the key. Anyway, I'd appreciate your help with the Oggs. For a start, coping with a new face will be good for them, and your friendly one is a bonus.'

I caught my reflection in the driver's mirror. I looked anxious, probably because the car's indicator was showing a right, meaning we'd probably be turning left. Keeping her options open and oblivious to the squealing brakes of a car coming behind, Sister Shiach was unperturbed. She maintained a steady course in the middle of the road and continued, 'Their baby's three months old now. Lovely wee fellow, if slow.' She cancelled the right-turn signal, then immediately turned into a street on the left. Her remark was casual. 'But that's what you'd expect of a mongol.'

The Oggs had a modern-built, smart-looking bungalow. It had such an immaculately tidy garden that the casual way my driver had parked her car in the driveway made the place look untidy.

'Somebody's seen us,' I said, glimpsing a pale face peeping out from behind a curtain.

It had gone by the time Sister Shiach waved. She said, 'That'll be Marion. I've told her we're coming. I've asked if her husband could be around too. I'm afraid they're both struggling to cope with this baby and they're wondering where they've gone wrong.' She bit her lip. 'And they won't want their neighbours seeing us visit. Let's catch them before they change their minds about letting us in.'

An anxious shadow was cast over Marion's pretty doll-like face as she opened the door then, glancing around as if to check whether anybody else was around, she ushered us in. 'Come in, quick, please! It's such a cold day.'

Sister Shiach dawdled, making a big play of wiping her feet clean. 'We don't want to bring dirty feet into the house,' she explained.

I could understand her reasoning. Waiting in the hallway I saw that all but one of the rooms leading off it had their doors open. Apart from the kitchen, they were carpeted in the same pale blue as where we stood. I presumed that the one with the closed door was the same. It must be murder to keep. I wondered what the Duthie brothers would make of something with a pile so thick they'd trip over it. No wonder Marion looked so anxious.

Rather more worrying, however, was the reason we were here. There didn't seem to be any sign of the baby. Where could he be?

There was one with a tear running down his cheek, only he was looking out from a Boots picture hanging on a white-painted wall. And from his viewpoint in the hall, there wasn't much to see, just a walnut sideboard standing on skinny legs.

From a quick glimpse through the open doors I saw only one bedroom. I wondered if it was the Oggs' and if they ever slept there. Its covers looked fresh out of the packet. The other rooms were as immaculate as a showroom exhibition. Bell's house with all its chaos felt more alive than this one with its air of vacancy and smell of beeswax.

A man, dwarfing Marion, appeared at her shoulder. They made a handsome couple, she with her fair good looks whilst he was tall and dark. 'Ah! Sister.' He glanced towards me, then added, 'Or should I say, Sisters, eh? Ha ha!' He rubbed his hands in a jovial fashion but his smile didn't reach his eyes and I sensed we weren't welcome.

Sister Shiach wasn't fazed. 'I've got an extra pair of hands just now so I thought I'd introduce you to Sister Macpherson. She's a modern miss – believes dads should have a hand in baby care.'

I nodded my head vigorously. 'It must double the pleasure whilst halving the work.'

'Ha ha! Halving work, eh? I could do with more than a half hand myself, and that's just for work. Dads helping? Crikey! Not always easy when you're already a working man, and self-employed at that.'

She might have the delicate look of a Christmas fairy but there was a note of steel in Marion's voice as, bending down to pick a thread off the carpet, she said, 'Well, but I do help you, Neil. Who keeps the house as well as doing your typing?'

Ignoring this, Mr Ogg bared his teeth and looked at his watch. 'Time's the thing, eh, Sister? Look at me. Already I've given up some of the valuable stuff just to meet up with you.'

Immune to his piercing blue eyes and chiselled jaw, Sister Shiach was forceful. 'Well, you're just lucky we've the time. Now I'd like a wee word with your wife. Sister here,' she said, nodding towards me, 'is going to help build up your confidence handling Andrew. He's old enough to cope with you bathing him now.' Taking Marion's arm, she steered her away from us. 'You go on, Neil. Take Sister Macpherson to see your son. I know you're both going to enjoy the training session.'

He threw his hands open and sighed in exasperation. 'Oh well, if you insist. But I hope this isn't going to take long.' Opening the previously closed door he waved me into the room as if he were a traffic policeman.

10

A FATHER'S ROLE

We were in a nursery with a military-looking Donald Duck marching across one of its lemon walls.

'Who's the artist?' I asked, wondering if I should step on or around the natural-coloured shag pile rug beside Andrew's cot. I looked down at the baby and saw an identical version of that boy in the Boots picture, except this one was asleep and had no tears.

'Marion. She knitted that too.' Mr Ogg nodded at a white and lemon crocheted cot blanket covering the baby. His laugh was bitter. 'She did it before he was born. Kept her options open as to the sex, but not for the fact it mightn't be normal.'

Usually mothers were shown how to bath their baby, either at their ante-natal classes or in the post-natal wards. Very few Sixties dads were offered the chance to get this experience and child rearing, in Dingwall at least, was still considered women's prerogative. Judging by his combative stance, Mr Ogg saw no reason to change the status quo.

Still, he was a captive audience and I couldn't have asked for a better-equipped place to give a demonstration. There was even a sink in the room. Next to it was a stand, holding a baby basin with enough towels and talcum powder in it to start a chemist's shop.

'Right,' I said, readying for work, 'let's waken our wee pal and see what he's to say for himself.'

Folding his arms and leaning against the door, Mr Ogg watched as I stroked Andrew's face and spoke to him, 'Morning, Wee Andrew. We've a special treat for you today. Your daddy's going to bath you. You'll need to be patient with him, mind. He's not very experienced.'

'I don't know why you're talking to him. You'll not get any response.' Mr Ogg spoke irritably.

'Oh, I dunno. Look.' I lifted Andrew out, and rubbing my cheek against his, heard his quiet breathing change. He gave a small cry. He had a shock of black hair, a perfect skin and until he opened his eyes, it would have been difficult to see he was different from any other baby.

His father backed away when I tried to hand him over. 'Oh, no – he just feels so floppy. I'm scared I'll drop him.'

'It's just because he hasn't the greatest of muscle tone. But that'll develop come time. You'll see. Go on.' I tried my most encouraging voice. 'Take him. I need to fill his bath. Show you what the right temperature is.'

'You're even bossier than Sister Shiach,' Mr Ogg complained, nevertheless taking off his jacket, draping it over a nursing chair then putting out his arms. 'Oh well, then!'

'Now chat to him, or sing,' I instructed. 'Babies like that.'

There was a lot of huffing and puffing until Mr Ogg realised he could use this heaven-sent opportunity to deliver a complaining message about interfering district nursing sisters without interruption. 'D'you know I think Andrew's listening,' he said with a note of wonder, then mischief. 'It must be because I'm talking such a lot of sense.'

'No. You're filling his head with nonsense. Now unless you were thinking of putting him in the bath with all his clothes on, you'll need to take them off,' I said, and threw a towel over the rug. 'Do it on this. It'll be safer.'

'It'll spoil my suit,' complained Mr Ogg, nevertheless getting down on his knees. 'Och, Andrew, she might have dimples, but underneath she's a hard woman.'

Andrew, released from his nappy, kicked as if in delight, but his father was morose.

'With legs like that you'll never be a sportsman.'

'I don't know about that,' I said, remembering someone I'd known who had a smile that embraced the world. 'We'd a boy like Andrew whose mum was our primary school's cleaner. She took him everywhere and he used to come to our school picnics. He won every race, fair and square. But nobody minded,' I thought back and smiled, 'probably because he always shared the sweetie prizes.

'What's more, he's still a lovely, happy chap,' I continued and swished the bath water. 'But come on, chaps, before this gets cold and, Andrew, who knows, one day you might become a top swimmer.'

'Not if I drown him first.' My pupil said as he advanced, holding his son with the tight control of a sumo wrestler. As Andrew squealed in protest, his father paled. 'See! I'm not the man for the job.'

'Och! That's just rubbish.' I said in exasperation. 'Hold him gently and look at him. Tell him what you're going to do. It's a well-known trick not doing something well so you can avoid doing it in future, but honestly, if you only do it the once you'll miss out on a whole lot of fun.'

He sighed. '"Fun," she says? All right. Whatever you say, Sister.'

'Put your hand under his furthest arm and keep a grip. That way you'll support his back and head and he won't slide under the water.' I spoke slowly.

A plainly nervous Mr Ogg snapped, 'I'm not stupid, you know.'

He held Andrew so that he was facing him. 'Well, son, are you ready for the big dip?' With immense care, he lowered him into the bath.

Our charge relaxed under the feel of the water and his fretful cries stopped. He looked thoughtful as his father gently splashed him, then gazing up at him he gave a gummy smile.

'Oh, my goodness! He likes that,' cried Mr Ogg, whilst a rogue tear sneaked down his face.

'Mission accomsplashed!' proclaimed my pupil. Leaving the nursery in a fine dusting of powder, we'd moved to the kitchen. It was a spotless chrome affair where both women were sitting at an island workstation.

'Which one of you had the bath?' Marion slid down from her high stool and in a fussy way tried to dust off the fine layer of Johnson's powder covering her husband's trousers. 'Just as well you took your jacket off.' She looked at him in disbelief as he jigged the baby.

'Andrew likes company in the water and Sister Macpherson says he probably likes it on dry land too. Ha ha!' he replied, now surely, genuinely smiling.

'That's true,' declared Sister Shiach. 'Nobody likes to be stuck on their own all the time. I think babies need to be where the action is. That's how they develop best.' She fished out her car keys and swung them before Andrew. 'And see how he's watching these? We might take everyday objects for granted, but this is his first time to see these, and look, already he's trying to grab them.'

'The consultant said he was a poor specimen.' Marion spoke in a wobbly voice. 'And not to expect too much of him.'

Sister Shiach's mouth tightened. 'I don't know how he could say that. We'll just have to prove him wrong. Wait till the pair of you get him out in his pram. You'll find nobody can resist this wee fellow!' She patted his thatch of black hair. 'But you'll need a bit more practice combing this lot before you go anywhere.'

'I forgot to do that,' said her husband, and pointing his finger at me, added, 'and so did somebody else.'

Marion wasn't ready for banter. She bit her lip and looked doubtful. 'Anyway, Neil, we wouldn't be going out in this weather.'

'But at least we could take in the pram – we could use it to walk Andrew around, but inside.'

'Inside?' Marion looked horrified. 'The pram'll take mud in on its wheels.'

'No it won't. I'll make sure they're clean. Anyway, it's never been used and the kitchen's easily big enough to take it,' Mr Ogg said, handing her the baby, 'but would you look at the time? I need to get to *proper* work now.' He nudged Sister Shiach in a teasing way. 'But before I do and to save you lot nagging, I'll get out the pram.'

'That's a good idea.' Sister Shiach was full of enthusiasm. 'And as your office is so near the toy shop you could pop in and buy pram beads. They're great entertainment for babies. Stimulating too. Sounds and colours make a great combination.'

She put a hand on Marion's arm. 'And having an occupied bairn will give you a bit of peace and allow you some time to do your typing for Neil. No reason why you can't do it at home, is there?'

'I suppose not,' Marion said, tapping her chin with a perfectly manicured fingernail. 'Sometimes I find it can be a long day, and housework's pretty boring after a while.'

'Trust me, you won't find it like that soon. Before long your son's going to get you both very busy, but happy. Don't forget that bit.' Sister Shiach climbed down from her stool and turned to me.

'Talking of work, we can't sit here all day. We've lots to get through before this afternoon's staff meeting.' She added with a touch of mischief, 'We'll be in the big meeting room at Council Headquarters and I hear the agenda includes a little drama. I'm looking forward to it and it should appeal to you, Sister Macpherson. Since you've arrived, there's been no shortage of it.'

11

A SEVERED HEAD

'Well in the end, the head had to be cut off.'

This surely couldn't be the little drama Sister Shiach had promised.

She'd just introduced me to a roomful of women, stout-clad in gabardine, sturdy shoes and all with the windblown, slightly weathered look of outdoor people. Their soft Highland-voiced welcome sounded genuine. I couldn't think that this group of kindly women wanted anything to do with violence. Settling back in their chairs they'd returned to everyday chat. Maybe they weren't aware of the more fascinating one going on in the row behind me. I stole a glance.

'Well, of course he was upset but it had to be done.' The tall grey-haired woman with a saint-like face spoke with authority. 'But I'll tell you about it later. Look, here comes Miss Macleod and fancy! Our Dr Duncan's here as well. Wonder what he's got to say.'

Her voice had turned frosty. It couldn't be for his lack of manners. Noticing that there was only one chair at the desk facing us, he escorted Miss Macleod to it in a courtly way. Once he'd made sure she was comfortably seated, he scurried off to get one for himself.

Team complete, Miss Macleod steepled her fingers, then,

viewing us with the approval of a benign headmistress, put her elbows on the desk and leant forward. 'We're so pleased that so many of you have managed to get here. I know it's not always easy what with your workload and having to cope with the bad weather and icy roads.'

She smoothed her hair (which hadn't a strand out of place) and took a deep empathising breath. It made the silver brooch on her jacket sparkle as if sending out a cheerful message, then she continued, 'But of course, we all need to keep up with our skills and medical knowledge. I'm sure you'll agree, Sister Mackay?' Miss Macleod arched her perfect eyebrows at my neighbour, who looked like a happy version of Sister Gall, except her hair was white, not grey, her cheeks pinker and her shoes an even shinier black.

'Well – yes, Miss Macleod, but I have to say that since our last meeting I'm *still* not happy about giving injections.' Her voice had a slight quaver whilst her hands twiddled with her coat buttons. 'You must understand, it wasn't part of our training in my day.'

Dr Duncan scraped back his chair and spoke irritably, 'Well you must appreciate by now times are changing, and fast. Medicine doesn't stand still and we all have to move with it.'

'I know you wanted me to practise, but putting a needle into the outer quadrant of an orange isn't the same thing at all at all. I'm running out of oranges and apples are out of season,' Sister Mackay protested, then, producing her killer line, she added, 'Anyway, I didn't become a nurse to inflict pain.'

'Nursing *Sister!*' Miss Macleod rapped her Conway Stewart pen on the desk. 'How many times have I to remind you?'

Sister Mackay ignored this but made an emphatic response. 'I was asked to give iron injections the other week. I couldn't sleep thinking about them. They're just horrible things to do.'

I thought about the big syringe full of black stuff injected into

Willie's flank, how it could stain the surrounding flesh if the original needle direction wasn't changed after insertion, and imagined he'd agree on the immediate unpleasantness. It was sometimes hard to convince a patient that, after all that, there would be an ultimate benefit.

The girl sitting on my other side now shot her hand up. 'I'm happy to help Sister Mackay with any injections she doesn't feel able to give. Her Munlochy patch is so close to mine in Avoch it'd be easy.' She smiled, and checked that her hat was still in place despite the exploding curls under it. 'And giving iron injections is hard.' She slapped her hip and grimaced. 'I certainly wouldn't fancy getting one.'

It was an unlikely possibility. She exuded health, energy and fun. When I first met her she collapsed in laughter when I called her Sister.

'Och, behave! It's Ailsa.' She had such a cheeky grin and vitality I imagined it'd be difficult for her patients to remember she'd any title other than her first name. I was also pretty sure that even if this was the case Ailsa still wouldn't want Miss MacLeod to know that.

The lady herself had meanwhile unsteepled her hands, leant back in her chair and went for a tone of sweet reason. 'Change is hard, I know that, but we can't ignore it, and if it improves the lot of patients then that's what we must work towards.' She cleared her throat, allowing Sister Mackay's small protests to die away, before continuing, 'One of the reasons we have these monthly meetings is so that we can keep abreast of medical matters. Dr Duncan has kindly come along today to give us some insight into diet and how it has a real influence on health.'

Dr Duncan stood up and looked about. By the sound of feet shuffling and the air of general restlessness, he might have gathered his audience wasn't totally engaged. I was surprised. He seemed a thoroughly decent, caring hard-working bloke and was – not that I was biased – an Aberdeen graduate.

'I know you'll want to be heading back to your homes before it gets dark,' he said, noticing a few heads turning towards the window, 'so let's get cracking.' He gave a dry laugh. 'Funnily enough, that's quite an apt introduction.'

He straightened his shoulders, checked his tie and gazed at something on the back wall. It must have fascinated him. He never took his gaze from it whilst he presented a case history of a man whose diet of eggs bumped up his cholesterol count until, said Dr Duncan in the voice of an undertaker, 'He died of a heart attack.'

After he'd finished there was a brief pause, then Ailsa leant back in her chair, crossed her arms, stretched out her legs and announced to the world in general, 'I'm not surprised that that bloke had a cardiac condition. I think he should've had his head examined as well. Fancy eating fourteen eggs a day!' Raising her index finger in the air, she made a corkscrew gesture. 'And you wouldn't have wanted to light a match near him either.'

'Quite,' said the doctor, almost relaxing at the sound of laughter, 'but you do see how too many eggs in the diet can be harmful. Sometimes it can just be too easy to use them instead of other more beneficial foods.'

Now he managed to directly address us. 'I'm sure you've come across patients who fit that category?'

There was a profound silence. Apparently everybody's patients led a dietetically perfect lifestyle.

'So no questions, then?' The doctor sounding relieved, got ready to leave, but then Sister Shiach stood up and in that artless, casual way she had of getting information other people might have to extract toenails to get, she said, 'Well, just before you go, there is one and I know it affects quite a few of us here.' She drew breath, ensuring she had an attention previously absent from the room, then continued, 'It's not really health-related but some of us have become rather anxious since we heard you were planning stopping us taking our dogs in our cars.' She gave a light laugh. 'Silly things, rumours, I know, but it would be nice for us if you could scotch this one.'

Ah! Now I saw the reason for the frosty reception. Dr Duncan obviously got the message because he went very pale. He took a handkerchief from his pocket and dabbed his mouth as if to stop it from speech. He darted a look at Miss Macleod, who suddenly seemed as fascinated by the blank wall as he had previously been.

'It's not actually a rumour,' he said. 'We're trying to encourage you all to use your own car if you have a dog. When we've gone to sell the County ones, we've found would-be buyers don't want either the smell of dog or their hair all over the car interiors.'

'But I need Dougie with me,' Sister Mackay burst out, 'he puts his paw on my arm whenever I go too fast.'

'That's true,' whispered Ailsa, 'I wouldn't get in her car without him.'

There was a storm of protest from the dog owners but Dr Duncan, making it clear the subject was closed, headed for the door.

'Just a moment,' Sister Shiach's voice, operating like a lasso, held fast the doctor. 'If that's the case, I've one more question and that is, if we haven't got our own cars already, can we expect help to buy one?'

He sighed and nodded his head. 'I thought you'd come up with something like that, Sister. So, yes, we can arrange a loan, but we don't want everyone asking for one at the same time.'

'Favourable rates?' Sister Shiach had apparently decided to pursue the matter to a conclusion.

Miss Macleod's voice cut in. 'Of course. I'll make sure of that. Now, we mustn't hold Doctor back. He's a busy man.'

'As if we're not,' said Ailsa. Ignoring this, Miss Macleod said, 'We'll have a short break then move on to the next part of our meeting. I've decided we'll have a little role play.' Responding to a bigger outbreak of discontented murmurs, she came back with a forceful, 'And I want you all to stay for that.' Then she accompanied the doctor out of the room.

As soon as they were gone, there was a general protest about nursing versus acting but that was nothing compared to the protests of the dog owners. There was a clamour of outraged voices. Suddenly there seemed to be two on-going dramas. But what about that severed head: was that not a third?

12

A LITTLE DRAMA
GOES A LONG WAY

I was determined to find out more about the missing head but couldn't. People only wanted to speak about dogs and cars, with Sister Mackay being particularly vocal. She dabbed her eyes with a lace-trimmed hanky, as she said, 'Look! We're a team, my dog and I, and my patients love Dougie. They want to see him more than me.' She sniffed and blew her nose. 'And he's a better tonic than any injection. Anyway, how could I afford a new car, and me so near retiring?'

Ailsa leant past me to pat her on the knee. 'Och, Daisy, you're always saying that but we all hope that's ages away. Anyway, you can't even get your work car on the Kessock Ferry 'cos that would take it out of Ross-shire. Your Munlochy patch is so close to Inverness it must be really frustrating seeing it just over the water. Why don't you apply for a loan? You could get a wee Mini.'

'A loan?' Sister Mackay was horrified. 'I wouldn't dream of it. That's debt!' She shuddered.

Ailsa looked thoughtful. 'Maybe I should get a dog and then I'd qualify to buy a car. Minis are cute and easy to drive and much better than the Morris Minors.' She pulled a face. 'People always recognise you in them.'

Sister Shiach stood up and all talk dropped away, the group giving her the respect accorded to a good shop steward. She said,

'Well, folks, I'm coming around to thinking that Dr Duncan's maybe got a point, so I'd consider applying for a loan. I could do with a bigger car. Obviously I could get more into it and that would suit me a lot better, *and* I bet I'd soon pay it off.'

She wagged a metronome-like finger at Sister Mackay. 'Now, Daisy, unless you've been squandering your money on the high living that the bright lights of Munlochy offer, you're bound to have a little savings put by.' Ignoring Daisy's squawk of protest, she continued. 'Just think, instead of you looking over the water, not only to Inverness but places like Ardersier and Nairn, you and Dougie could nip over and have your day off there. Think how he'd enjoy that —a change of air would do you both good. Fresh horizons. That's great for a dog.'

It was a clever move and by the time Miss Macleod came back, people had begun to think that car ownership might after all have some merit. On the other hand, the proposed role play continued to get a lukewarm response, with a lot of people saying they needed to get their work done before it was dark and bad weather stopped them from getting home.

Miss Macleod smiled gently. 'Uh uh.' She shook her head. 'We've got a little time left. Yes, really. You know it's only too easy, as I keep stressing, to let professional standards slip. So you're all going to stay and accept the fact that role play's an ideal tool for learning.'

In the manner of somebody who might relish a spot of gladiatorial sport, she continued, 'As we all know, a new staff member has joined us. What you mightn't know is that Sister Macpherson's unsure about doing health visiting without qualification. Of course, if we lived in a perfect world, all our staff members would be suitably trained when they start. But until then we have to rely on our unqualified sisters to use their common sense.'

She spread her arms wide then clapped her hands together and all but said, *Abracadabra*. Instead, she added, 'So taking part in role play might be just the thing for giving her confidence. I think if she takes the role of a health visitor dealing with a difficult mother it could be very instructive.' She turned her gaze on Ailsa. 'For this to be credible we need someone around Sister Macpherson's own age to act as her patient, so I guess that has to be you.'

Torn between resentment at the ageist remark and relief that they hadn't been chosen, the rest of the group turned their eyes towards Ailsa, who flung her hand to her brow in a prima donna fashion. 'Oh well, I suppose, if I must!' She got up, slung off her coat, grabbed her scarf, and sticking out her tongue at Daisy, headed for the door. 'I'll need a moment or two to get in the mood.' As she tossed her head back and left, I thought she sounded quite pleased. Maybe being classed as young, or perhaps playing at being a difficult mum, appealed.

I hadn't expected this. Perhaps I should have guessed, but only now did I realise what Sister Shiach had meant about drama. She was pals with Miss Macleod. I bet they'd planned this long before the meeting.

My heart sank. The last time I'd done role play was with a group of fellow students in our general student nurse training days. We were supposed to be treating our 'patient' for an asthmatic attack. Painting our pal's face with gentian violet to convey heart and breathing distress had seemed like a good idea at the time, as had been the cameo appearance of an enema funnel and tube. If she hadn't escaped our caring clutches and been given a whiff of oxygen, our acting patient could easily have become a real one. Our tutors gave us a terrible row. Since then, I'd given role play a wide berth.

'Whilst we're waiting for Sister, has anybody any special experience they want to share?' Miss Macleod wondered aloud. 'It's always interesting to hear about other people's work.'

I was sure the severed head story would provide a welcome distraction, but the teller didn't oblige. Instead, she said, 'If our two colleagues are any good at acting I'll be able to recommend them to James Robertson Justice. You know, he plays Sir Lancelot Spratt in the *Doctor* films?'

'Oooh, yes!'

After the admiring chorus died down, she laughed. 'Well, nobody can say our working lives are dull. I once attended him at his Spinningdale home. He made me feel as if I was on set when he breezed towards me, rubbing his hands and shouting, "Good Morning, Sister!" D'you know, I came away from there thinking I was a real film star.'

'I'd be better pleased if it was Dr Sparrow. That Dirk Bogarde who plays him is just lovely,' mused Daisy. 'Och! If only I was younger.' She started as Ailsa floated into the room. 'Losh! That can't be Ailsa? My goodness. She's turned into one of yon funny folk. Hippies, I think they call them.'

Ailsa was bare-footed and wore a long, flame-coloured cardigan which swamped her dress. She'd swapped her hat for a yellow scarf, which she'd turned into a bandana.

'She must have borrowed those from Big Susan the receptionist. She goes in for bright colours,' Daisy noted, consulting her shoes and tapping them together approvingly, and just before she gave an affronted, 'Well!'

Ailsa had held up two fingers. They could easily have been misconstrued if she hadn't then waved them before her like windscreen wipers. 'Peace, my sisters,' she chanted. Miss Macleod had joined the rest of the audience so as Ailsa took her chair she held out a beckoning finger in my direction and pointed to Dr Duncan's. 'Sit down, Sister. Oh, you must!'

In the manner of a respectful caller, I did, whilst she continued in a voice so breathless you'd have thought she'd run up three flights of stairs. 'Thanks so for visiting. I've actually been expecting you to call for a few days now. How nice you've managed it – eventually. Of course, I'd heard you've just arrived and it's quite wonderful to see such a young face.' She leant and said in a stage whisper, 'Being new to any community can be lonely but I'm actually given to understand you've not been quite alone.' She gave an exaggerated wink.

I didn't need to be an actress to look perplexed and settled for clearing my throat. What was she on about?

Ailsa was happy to elaborate. 'Ha ha! I hear my neighbours talking about seeing a man's underwear on your washing line but,' she said, patting her front proudly, 'I personally salute you for braving the gossips.'

Planning to kill Ailsa afterwards and noting that my house, even if it was in a cul-de-sac in a small village, didn't guarantee privacy, I managed an even tone. 'Yes. I've found that's the wonderful thing about living in a community. Everybody takes a great interest in each other. I think it's because they care.'

Ailsa bent her head as if to pick a thread off the bottom of her cardigan. 'Fifteen all,' she muttered. Then, straightening up, she gushed, 'Oh, Sister, I so agree. Peace and harmony's so important.' She drew breath, then went on, ' Now I realise you've been so busy settling in you haven't *made* the time to visit little old me, but I have actually been rather anxious to get some help. This being my first little cherubeee and all.' She clasped her head and bent low as if in pain.

Ailsa's sudden imitation of distress could have won her an Oscar. I leant forward and covered her hand. 'I know new babies bring a whole change of lifestyle, but is there a particular problem?'

'It's the . . .' She put her hand to her mouth as if to tell a secret but actually magnified her voice. It made the sound bounce off the walls. 'Sex! My husband's most insistent.'

I nearly asked her to repeat herself but thought better of it. A small ripple of disapproving 'tuts' swept the room. It was obvious from everybody's rapt attention that they had all heard her complaint and by the way they were all craning forward, wanted to hear more.

Whilst Daisy had gone even pinker than Ailsa's cardigan, I noticed Miss Macleod cross her legs and raise one eyebrow. A smile flickered.

I decided on a direct approach. 'So how old's the baby?'

Ailsa had such a gleam in her eye I'd have wagered she'd say a week. Instead, she went for three weeks. 'I didn't want to ask the last nurse. I thought I might shock her, but pardon me for saying this, Sister, but you're *quite* young. You might understand sex matters better.'

'Thanks, Ailsa,' I could have said. Instead, remembering some fairly robust conversations with Belfast fathers during my midwifery training, I soldiered on. 'I've found it sometimes helpful for dads to meet us. Then we can discuss this sort of thing together – and probably best to do it sooner than later, eh?' I looked at my watch.

'Okay. Great!' Ailsa dived into her pocket and took out a piece of paper. 'Excuse me a moment.' She made a great show of rolling then sucking on it. She blew an imaginary cloud of smoke into my face, meanwhile giving me a measured look. 'This keeps me chilled. I hope you don't mind.'

I waved my hand and started coughing, really getting into the part. 'Sorry. It's my weak chest, you see. My mother used to smoke all the time and it made me vulnerable to any kind of smoke and, of course, that's what gave her terrible bronchitis. But of course you'll know how defenceless babies are. You won't be smoking near yours, will you, and where's the wee one, by the way?'

Ailsa looked about her in an astonished way, as if she had forgotten she had one. 'He's about to waken up, I should think.'

'And how are you feeding him?'

Making a show of stubbing out her fag, Ailsa stood up. She stretched out her arms as if to embrace the world. With a cry that might have alerted the emergency services had we been in hospital, she shouted, 'Breast!'

The cardigan was swept apart like curtains being opened. I fully expected a full frontal. Instead, Ailsa's blue frock took centre stage and with a groovy move she crooned, 'Yeah, my Sister, you gotta dig it. Breast sure is best.'

After a stunned silence there was a burst of applause and Miss Macleod stood up. 'Well,' she said, 'I don't know about education, but that was certainly entertaining, and if you do have a hippy or two on your district, you might well be prepared for a similar conversation.' She glanced out of the window then, finally acknowledging the gathering dusk, said, 'You'll all be wanting to get home but just before you go, has anyone some brief advice for Sister Macpherson?'

'Yes, I have,' said a familiar voice from the back. 'I've a warning and it's that crofters can be a fly breed. They watch their pennies and most of them don't want to call out a vet when they think a nursing sister will do instead. I'd a call from a shepherd yesterday. He'd a lambing with twins that came together. The live one couldn't get out for the other one, which was dead with its head stuck in the birth canal. Because I'd hate to think of anything suffering I did make a visit but it was all a bit traumatic.' She bit her lip and looked upset. 'All I'm going to say is, I'm glad the man had a sharp blade. He just needed me to tell him to use it.'

13

SOLE OPERATOR

Remembering Dr Duncan's lecture, I thought that without Willie to cook for him Jock might resort to an egg-alone diet. Perhaps I should warn him he might disappear in a cloud of sulphur or simply drop dead.

He was shutting in the hens for the night. As they settled on their roosts, their squawks died to a croon and sounded as comforting as Jock. 'Eggs, you say? Och, you've no need to worry. The poor things are off the lay.'

He must have got his bonnet back from Willie. He took it off, scratched his head, then pointing to its egg-shaped dome, said, 'But I'll show the hennies this and it'll maybe remind them to get back to work.' His smile was brave, but he faltered a bit, saying, 'An' when the bonny days come the hennies'll be sure to get back to the lay and by then surely Willie will get home home.'

He didn't look convinced as I protested, 'He'll be back long before then. Hospitals don't want folk taking up beds forever and I bet he'll be planning menus in his chair in front of his own fireside before you can say you're hungry. Unless of course you've heard otherwise.' I gazed around at a wintry scene. 'You not having the phone, how would you know?'

Jock nodded at his bike. It had the sleek class of a Raleigh, somewhat marred by that awful old hat, back to covering the seat.

'I biked in this afternoon.' He sucked his teeth and shook his head. 'He's on the mend and liking hospital – especially the tellyveesion.' Mournfully, he continued, 'Now, with all those comforts he mightna want to come home. D'you know what he was telling me, Nursie?' His eyes widened into pale blue orbs.

'What?' I asked, thinking that Willie's spell in hospital must have restored his voice as well as his temperature.

'He says they're talking of landing men on the moon. The moon! I was sure he was havering but the nurses said not.' He drew breath. 'But why would anybody want to be doing that?' He scratched his brow in bewilderment. 'When they get there, they'll only fall doon on the ground. And Willie says it'll be on the telly.' He tried out the word in a wondering way. 'The telly.'

We looked up at a sky where the moon, unaware it was soon to have visitors, was serenely sailing.

Jock was beginning to get into his stride. 'You know yon manny they talk about here – the Brahan Seer? Kenneth Mackenzie was his real name but they cry him after Brahan Castle, where he was a labourer. The castle's been demolished but it's where the Big Hoose is now.' He jerked his head sideways. 'The Seer's long gone but he's famous for foretelling things.' He tapped my arm. 'And some of it's come true. But he never said anything about men on the moon.' Jock shook his head in amusement. 'So I'll believe it when I see it. Anyway, we're no getting a telly, a telly.'

'But I've heard he prophesised black rain too,' I chuckled, all too unaware that oil finds would soon transform this part of the world. Who'd have dreamt the Firths would be surrounded by fabrication yards building oil rigs to drill for the black stuff the seer apparently had predicted?

'Just goes to prove you shouldn't believe everything you hear,' I added.

'Same goes for eggies,' Jock managed a twinkle. 'Don't you

worry about me, Nursie, the farm folk have said that if I give them a hand, they'll make me food to take home and maybe they'll manage the odd denner too, denner too.'

I left him gazing heavenward and wondered was it my imagination or was Jock repeating himself less frequently. I headed for home. I was hoping to find the same level of comfort there as Jock's hens heading for their roosts, and I might have broken into a cluck myself had it not been for those wretched long johns. As if highlighting the freedom of a moon riding the skies, they hung, damp and tethered in as disconsolate a way as they'd jigged so joyously before.

Pulling them off the washing line, I said, 'You're sullying my reputation. Come inside at once and get properly dry. You're going home soon, and that's a promise.'

Despite my brain registering the middle of the night, my watch insisted it was seven a.m. whilst the owner of the wakening voice at the end of the phone said she was Ann, Muir of Ord's Sister. She sounded anxious. 'Sorry to wake you so early but Miss Macleod asked me to give you a call. You see, my mother's taken ill and she's been rushed to hospital in Perth. She lives near there. I need to get down as quick as possible.' There was a pause then she said in a small voice, 'So could you manage to fill in for me?'

I remembered her from yesterday's meeting where I'd found her gentle, spinsterish way a little more predictable than Ailsa's mischievous one. I suspected that with her level of quiet self-containment she'd have found it difficult asking for help.

'Certainly. I'd be delighted.' That was true. Already I was out of bed, taking instructions and feeling excited. Even though Muir of Ord was Ann's district, I'd be their nurse until she came back.

She continued, 'There's a diabetic needs insulin. His name's Mr Munro and he's due his injection at half past eight. Could you make that? If you can it'd give me time to catch the bus into Inverness so I can get the Perth connection. I'll leave the house key at the back door.'

'Is he on his own?'

'No. Lives with his wife. They're a sweet old couple. Retired from crofting. You'll enjoy meeting them.' She went on, 'I suppose you should go on using your relief car rather than the one that's here.' She clicked her teeth. 'It annoys me to see this one just sitting there and going nowhere when I could have jumped into it and been off. Uh! It would be so much easier if we had our own cars. Dogs or no bally dogs.'

Amused, if surprised by her direct tone, I said, 'Well, it's no problem this end of the line and Muir of Ord's really close. I'll be there in a jiffy. Just keep in touch and let us know how things are with both you and your mum.'

I'd hoped to sound reassuring, but she was gone and I had to get to Muir of Ord quick. All I needed to do now was to leave a forwarding address on the answering machine.

The previous night was the first time I'd used one. It was huge and seemed to have more buttons than a cardiac monitor. Still, I'd had fun pressing the record knob and singing into the microphone. Confident I'd mastered the technology and sure that my bawdy ballad-rendering had been replaced with cool and clear details as to my whereabouts, I headed for Ann's house at Muir of Ord.

I didn't want a patient with a diabetic coma to be the first casualty of the day but there was one of another kind already waiting at Ann's house. 'You'll find a note of my week's work in the office beside the green book and phone, and maybe you should check for any messages,' she'd said.

When I got there, a red light was blinking on the answering machine. I pressed the 'play' button and nearly jumped out of my skin. Right away I turned down the volume, scared that if the Muir of Ord folk heard Miss Macleod's bellowing voice, they'd be thrown into as big a state of alarm as myself.

'I've just called you at your house and heard your message on the answering machine. How dare you!' There was a brief silence as if she was too shocked to speak, but then she continued, 'There were two totally unsuitable messages on it. I was shocked by both. The first one was bad enough. I've never heard a ruder song. What kind of thing's that to leave on any phone, never mind one belonging to a supposed professional and then, as if that wasn't bad enough—' There was another silence. I twiddled the volume knob but it made no difference. Her voice came back, full-boom. 'You've referred to yourself as Nurse Macpherson on the other message. *Nurse!* You'll just get back and change that message as soon as possible. It's not the sort of thing I ever want to hear again. D'you hear me, *Sister?*'

The message ended as she slammed down her phone.

I felt thoroughly chastened and wondered if she had heard Miss Macleod would Ann have let me loose in Muir of Ord? Her office spoke order and efficiency. Antiseptic Savlon and Eusol bottles were lined up with military precision on a shelf where they shared space with swab packs and cotton wool. The nursing bag stood on its own.

Ann must have spent hours polishing it for it had such a gleam it could have put Daisy's shiny shoes to shame. There was enough equipment inside the bag to cope with a nuclear fallout, with the instruments glittering like a canteen of prize cutlery. The bag was very unlike my own third-hand, battered model. Hoping it would convey a suitable degree of efficiency and professionalism, I grabbed it and got back into my car.

Ann's directions were clear and Muir of Ord not very big so finding Mr Munro, my diabetic patient, was easy. I wondered how he'd react to getting treatment from such a disgrace to the profession.

Glumly, I parked the car. At least I was in time, with his wife, obviously on the lookout, answering the door at my first knock.

I explained Ann's absence and that I was her substitute. Despite the fact that there was nobody around, Mrs Munro spoke at a run, as if she needed to get her message over before being interrupted. 'Come away, come away. Himself's in the kitchen, aye, waiting for you – well we've both been.' She wore a flowery-patterned apron and wiped one hand on it before shaking mine. 'Oh! Mind it's maybe not very clean. I've just been scrubbing the sink all ready for Sister Ann. And now it's you. Well that's a surprise, I can tell you.' She bustled ahead, pulling at her clothes then patting them to check all was in place. A faint smell of bleach hung in her wake.

The Munros might be retired but Mrs Munro had the voice and laugh of a young girl. I was supposed to be the cheerful and bright one but she was much better at it. Now mischief dimpled her rosy cheeks. 'We're always thinking Sister Ann might surprise us all one day and just elope. She's a bonny, kind lassie and would make a great wife.'

Miss Macleod might not have approved of an inference that *Mrs* was the only title worth having, but then Mrs Munro continued with a laugh, 'And we'd be the worse off for losing her. Look how she's got us to set out your stuff, eh, Angus?'

A tall man, as thin as his wife was plump, got up from the table where a white plastic tray was laid out with an insulin vial, medical wipe, small forceps in a bowl of Savlon and a spotlessly white huckaback towel. He spoke with a soft Isle of Lewis accent, and whilst his outstretched hand felt work-rough in mine, he had the grave manner of a thinker. He said, 'Aye, Sister Ann's so organised I'm thinking we could maybe do surgical operations here as well. That would give us a bit of excitement. Sometimes it can get a wee bit monotonous round here.'

He sat down, straight-backed, and gazed at the tray with such a serious look that for a moment I thought he was going to say grace.

A pan made a clattering sound from the stove. 'Would you be hearing that?' he said. 'We're boiling a syringe and a needle! *Smaoinich* (imagine)! I'm thinking I'm no needing all of this. Sister's maybe a bit too organised. It was never like this when I was injecting the sheep, and I never heard any of them complaining.'

Mrs Munro flapped a dishtowel at him. 'Angus! Operations, is it? Well I never! Not once did you manage to put a needle in any animal – not in all your life. No! That was always left to me. And why, Sister?' Angus looked slightly hang-dog whilst his wife ran on, "Cos himself here faints at the sight of blood.' Her eyes sparkled and she threw her head back and laughed. 'So what do you say to that, Sister?' Without waiting for a reply, she sped on. 'Whoever said a shepherd's wife had an easy life must have been joking, that's what I say and always have done.'

'Nonsense, woman. You needed something to do,' said Angus, nevertheless turning his head as I used the forceps to fish out the syringe and needle, assembled them then gave him his injection. 'Anyway, I don't know why you're complaining. You women have it easy compared to those ones.' He nodded at a framed, sepia-tinted photograph hanging on the wall. Black-clad, head-squared women, backs laden with peats, grimaced into the camera.

'Right enough,' said his wife with just a hint of malice, 'and you'd probably be dead, and not through hard work either.'

He gave a sigh. It had all the pathos of a Hebridean lament. 'I'm proper useless though and it's a long day for somebody used to always being on the go. A crofter's life doesn't train you for retirement.' He banged his hand on his knee in frustration.

'Well, I've plenty to do,' declared Mrs Munro, handing me the towel to dry my hands. As soon as I'd finished, she slung it into a basin reeking of bleach. 'Oh, it's busy I am! I've never time on my hands.'

Days of disposable syringes and needles weren't far away, solving many of her problems, but the modern method of finger pricking to test for blood sugar might not have held the same appeal to Angus. He seemed coy enough about the existing method of urine testing. 'There's the results,' he'd murmured, showing me a chart which had been carefully filled in to show his urine had been tested and was sugar free.

Reassured that I'd given him the right dosage, I left the Munros enjoying their cheerful banter and headed for Miss Forbes, my next patient.

She lived nearby in a Dorran bungalow. When I saw its garden gate hanging drunkenly on one hinge I thought anyone could have wandered in, but soon realised few would want to. A huge holly tree almost blocked entry to a wild unkept garden with overgrown bushes making a territorial bid for the cobbled path leading to the house, beside which a snowberry bush flourished. Its white berries hung on thread-like branches, giving it a skeletal shape. The whole made a mockery of the house's Rose Cottage name.

Ann's list said Miss Forbes had congestive cardiac failure and needed general nursing care. Her problem made it difficult for her to get up, to wash, dress and manage everyday chores herself. Ann's notes had included the comment, 'Dog a hazard and a very proud patient' and although I should have taken this more seriously, I was prepared for the dog. Holding the nursing bag in front of my legs and ankles, I knocked at the door then opened it.

A thing with all the appeal of an old string floor mop came charging towards me. Had it not been moving forwards I might still not have known which end was which, but the teeth left no doubt. They were small but bared, yellow and now slavering over a mouthful which could have been me had it not been for the stout leather bag.

'Down, you ugly brute!' I roared. 'Get down!'

The thing skidded to a halt, back legs meeting the front ones. It whined, then with its tail tucked between its legs slunk back to what I presumed was the living room. I followed and watched as it squeezed under a camp bed that was so low it was surprising anything could get under it.

'Don't speak to LBP like that. She wouldn't harm a fly. I think you've hurt her feelings. And who are you, anyway?' The voice came from the bed. Although it was weakened by breathlessness, it still held a command I recognised.

Memories of camping with a group of other Girl Guides in a field near Muir of Ord came flooding back. I looked again, suddenly remembering that this Miss Forbes had come to inspect how the camp was being run. Impressive in her uniform and with a gash of lipstick, the only feminine concession to her military bearing, she strode around inspecting patrols, checking our ties for their knots, our badges for their polish. Her experience as a district commissioner had given her the ability to carry her message over a twelve-acre field. At a jamboree, she must have struck terror into all those girls who failed to appreciate the fun of survival games played in the great outdoors. Heaven help those guides at a more local, smaller event she held responsible for loose guy ropes and wrongly-angled tent pegs.

Now, however, with her powers sadly diminished, she lay under a heap of blankets covered in dog hair, no help to her breathing problems. I wanted to check her pulse but she was wearing so many layers of clothes it couldn't be done unless she allowed it. Right now, this seemed unlikely. Maybe, as that Raigmore doctor had hinted, it was easier dealing with unconscious patients.

A cold draught blew round my ankles, and still worried about LBP taking a bite out of them, I made my introduction brief.

Miss Forbes struggled to sit up and then adjusted her hairnet. I wondered if it was the same one (as I recalled her saying) that only came off was when she was putting up a bell tent. Now, less efficiently, it sat over her eyebrows whilst she dealt out a measuring look.

'Sister, you say? Young whipper-snapper, more like. Anyway, I don't think you're a very nice sort of person. Look how you shouted at LBP and came barging in here.' She patted her chest as if that might help her breathing, then managed to wheeze, 'So I think you should take your little black bag and get out before I call my doctor and tell him there's a cheeky young brat here masquerading as a nurse and certainly not a Sister.' She slid down the bed again. 'So thank you for calling but goodbye.'

I felt like the naughtiest girl in the patrol and wondered how Sister Shiach would have coped with the situation. Probably by this time, I thought miserably, she'd have had LBP enrolled in a 'better-manners' course run by Jomo. Meanwhile, Miss Forbes would be happy, chatty, washed, dressed and sitting with a cup of tea in front of a cheery fire reminiscing on how three sharp whistle blasts could alert help from every guiding corner.

Clearly, I'd upset both my patient and her dog. I stood for the moment, undecided. Miss Forbes was giving a very good impression of being fast asleep, whilst LBP's nose stuck out from under the bed as if she were on sentry duty. She must think I'm a threat to both her mistress and herself, I thought, and only a bucket-load of tact and diplomacy will put things right.

Compared with Raigmore's standard lightweight model, the commode near the bed was a substantial affair of mahogany-coloured wood. The Queen Anne legs added class. The back and pan lid were padded in rich red velvet. I sat down on the lid, hoping that it was as solid as the rest of the chair.

If Miss Forbes had been taking her diuretic tablets the pan would need emptying, but she was so breathless I suspected she hadn't been. It seemed more likely that her body was holding such a build-up of fluid it was putting pressure on both her heart and lungs.

LBP's nose, on very active duty, inched out a little further.

I tried for a conciliatory tone, 'You're a good dog, LBP, and I'm very sorry if I've offended you.'

She looked doubtful. Nevertheless, she managed to squeeze her head out sideways, which made it as unbecoming as her accompanying growls and snarls.

I went on, 'But, for a lady, your language is unbecoming and, frankly, I think your namesake, would be horrified by it. Lady Baden-Powell had very high standards.'

As if I'd sounded a reveille, there was a stirring under the blankets. Miss Forbes shot open her eyes and gave me a look that was more curious than suspicious.

'Do I take it you were a guide?'

'I certainly was. I loved being one.' Remembering growing up on a Highland upland farm where cats and dogs constituted high society, I was honest. 'If it hadn't been for guiding I don't think I'd be where I am today.' I recognised that my present position might not be regarded as the high point of a career, so I hurried on. 'What I mean is that I learnt from people who were dedicated to giving young folk the benefit of their time and experience, that there's an exciting world beyond home ground and that it's well worth exploring.'

'And did you learn how to make a cup of tea?' Miss Forbes wondered.

'Yes, and how to light a fire. Come on, LBP, you can show me where the sticks are.'

Encouraged by her mistress's tone of voice, LBP made her full appearance. She might have had an ancestry of Westie Scottish terrier blend but now, grey-haired, whiskery and dishevelled, she was more like a pocket edition of Miss Forbes. Still, she didn't have swollen legs or a hairnet. The latter would have helped to hold back the long fringe obscuring her view. Perhaps her mistress wasn't seeing too well herself. I was sure she'd have been vexed if she'd realised LBP had matted bits on her coat and nails that were too long. They clicked on the linoleum as she followed me into the kitchen.

There was a whistling kettle on a solid Baby Belling ring. It looked as if it might achieve blood heat, if we lived long enough. The outside back door stood open.

'There's a flask of hot water on the table, and the tea caddy's on the window sill,' my patient instructed, her voice rising marginally. 'That cooker takes as long to heat up as it does to cool down so I try to use what they call its residual heat.' She gave a derisory snort. 'Supposed to save energy. Whose, I wonder.'

A smiling Queen graced the tea caddy with a red geranium standing beside it bursting with health in stark contrast to a back garden so overgrown that LBP, who'd gone out the open door, had completely disappeared.

I was a bit anxious about her, but Miss Forbes was reassuring. 'She'll be all right. The back garden's secure. That's why I leave the door open. She can come and go at will. It's not always easy for me to get to it.'

Her admission that she had a difficulty emboldened me.

'Would you think of having someone in to give you a hand. Maybe a home help?'

There was such a long pause that I thought she must either have fainted or that my supposed tact and diplomacy were being given due consideration.

14

POULTRY MANAGEMENT

The silence was actually Miss Forbes needing all her energy to get out of bed. It was so low she merely rolled out onto the floor. However, it wasn't going to be so easy getting up from there. I tried to help but she shrugged me off. 'Leave me. Once I roll over, I'll get onto my knees.'

It was hard standing by, just watching, but she persevered. Eventually she managed, then, using the commode arms as leverage, she pulled herself up. As soon as she did, she plumped down on the commode seat, exhausted and wheezing so badly I wondered if I should call her doctor.

There was a telephone beside a stack of *The Guide* magazines on the kitchen table. I checked the line was operational, then fiddled about a bit, hoping to give Miss Forbes time to recover at her own pace.

Eventually when I did go back, she said, 'For goodness' sake, don't look so worried. From the way you're looking, you'd think I was about to keel over.' She was still breathless but she managed, 'I expect it looks much worse for you. Actually, I was up a few times last night. I'm sure that's making me more chesty than usual. I'll get better as the morning goes on. I always do.' She tried to inhale, but stopped short. 'But as you're there, you could help me put on my dressing gown.'

It was a small concession that I was useful, and I was even more pleased when she followed it up with, 'You know, it's not that I wouldn't like a bit of help, it's just that I hate upsetting LBP. She's timid but she's got it into her foolish head that I need to be protected. It puts her on red alert all the time. That's not good for any caller or a dog. I do worry about her especially now that I'm not so able to exercise her. At least she's getting that free run outside. That's why I leave the door open. She can come and go as she likes. Plenty of fresh air's good for the two of us, I say!'

From the blood-curdling growls and snarls floating through the door, I figured that, at the very least, LBP's lungs were beneficiaries.

'She won't get out the front, will she?' I asked, remembering the broken gate.

'No. The back's blocked off. It's a pity. She'd have even more space then, but I wouldn't want her run over. We're so near the road a car could easily get her. Now once I get that cup of tea, I'll get washed and dressed and then I'll see if you can light a fire with only one match. Mind, I'll be watching!'

Was there humour in that voice, I wondered, handing over tea in an enamel cup, the only one I could find without turning the kitchen upside down. Miss Forbes plunged her hand into the dressing gown pocket and took out a bottle of tablets.

'These damn water pills make me pass enough to sink a ship,' she said, 'but at least I'm up now and able to make the loo – so much better than this thing.' She wrinkled her nose and banged the commode's arms. 'I never did like latrines.'

As she took a tablet with her last swallow of tea, I blurted out, 'That should help your breathlessness too.'

'I'm not that,' she wheezed. 'I'm just fine. I'll manage the rest myself, and once that fire's got going so can you. I'm sure you've plenty others to see to. We'll see you tomorrow.'

* * *

Snow fell, feathering the windscreen. As I got into the car, I worried about Miss Forbes. At least, I supposed, she'd let me help her get washed and dressed to sit by the fire. I'd even made my peace with LBP, now happily sitting on her mistress's knee. My patient was so independent she was never going to really admit her problems, but if this cold continued, by tomorrow morning I might have another Willie scenario, only there'd be a rabidly protective dog to deal with as well.

At the time of my visit, I'd wondered why Miss Forbes was in such an unsuitable bed, but a sneak peek had shown that she couldn't get near any other. Every room was crammed with guiding paraphernalia she was plainly unable to sort. Pride was an issue. So was confidentiality.

It might be easier to keep in Muir of Ord, divided by a busy main road, but villages are prized for neighbourly interest. Miss Forbes mightn't see it like that. Maybe I could ask Ann if she knew anyone who was discreet, a dog-handler, had guiding experience and an ability to empathise with a proud old lady, now frail and fallen on hard times.

The anxiety chewed away at the back of my mind through a morning dealing with Ann's list and reassuring her patients that I wasn't a permanent replacement. As soon as was possible, I drove back to Conon Bridge so that I could leave a politically correct message on the answering machine. Then there were the long johns. They needed to get back to their owner. I'll pop them in to Jock, I thought. It won't take a minute.

It was as startling to see a television aerial sprouting from the Duthie house as it was to hear flapping noises coming from the tree beside it. Two hens were perched on a branch halfway up it. Resisting Jock's attempts to coax them down, they merely spread out their wings for balance, clucking irritably as if annoyed at being disturbed.

'Come on, Dilly and Dally. Get down out of there. The other hens won't touch you.' Jock rattled a pail of grain which mightily interested every hen but those in the tree.

With no sign of the pair moving and the defiant squawks continuing, I was reminded of LBP. The attitude was much the same. I nearly suggested chucking a brick at them but then remembered Jock's soft heart. I couldn't think how else to help. Still, it was an intriguing situation, so I went for, 'I didn't know any of your hens had names.'

'The Campbells gave them to me. They said I'd need eggs for Willie for when he comes home and these are good layers.' Jock didn't sound convinced. 'The bairns had them for pets but got scunnered of them. The Campbells are awful soft, you know. They just left that two to please themselves.' He glared up at the tree. 'And that bit's true. I should never have let them out of that box.' He kicked the one lying at his feet. 'It'll serve them right if they freeze up there. Just look at the other hens, they've all gone inside. Now that's girls with common sense, common sense!'

'And that should apply to us too.' I handed over the long johns, which Jock took and tucked under his arm in an absent-minded sort of way.

'Fine, fine,' he said. 'Willie was asking about them. I'll get them to him this afternoon.' He returned his gaze to the tree. 'Once I get Dilly and Dally down.'

I shivered. There were flakes of snow sliding down the back of my neck and my chilblains itched.

'You're not biking in?'

It must be especially cold. Jock was wearing a raincoat. Compared to the rich red-brown of those pesky Rhode Islands, it was more like the colour of mud. As he tightened the belt, he threw me a challenging look. 'Of course. Willie'll be looking for me.'

I remembered Sister Shiach and the old man she worried about falling off his bike. Ann's list of afternoon work was short and I didn't want to start worrying about Jock as well as Miss Forbes. Then too, being a compassionate sort of person, I thought about my poor feet. They deserved a decent pair of boots. I could maybe buy them ones in Dingwall.

'Look. I'll take you in.'

You'd have thought it was an indecent proposal. 'Oooh, no! I'll manage fine.' He said, then looking worriedly at Dilly and Dally. 'I'm running short of time though and you'll be wanting to get on with your work, Nursie, Nursie.'

The snowflakes now melting and making a chilly track down my back made me irritable. 'That's true and this is holding me up so look, Jock, I'll make a deal with you. I've got to go to Dingwall anyway, so if I help you get those brats down will you let me drive you there?' Not waiting for an answer, I looked around. 'Have you a ladder?'

Torn between care for Willie and caution regarding transport, Jock had decided that in the meantime, he'd be safe enough with a ladder. He came back with a metal one, evidently stored at the back of the house.

'Man's work,' he said, leaning it against the tree then clearing the rungs of snow, 'but maybe you could steady it.'

Continuing their stance, the hens looked down, shouting in defiance and spreading their wings as if readying for take-off. Still, I reckoned they looked safer than Jock. As he started to climb, his tackety boots clinked on the rungs. Occasionally there was a scrape as his foot slipped. Never had such roadman-like noises sounded so dangerous. A cold hand clutched my heart. I held onto the ladder like grim death. What if he fell?

Nurse training, like a few other things I was discovering on district, hadn't catered for poultry management or immediate care of somebody flattened by a falling person. As I looked up at those

94

trouble-making hens, I thought back to my farm childhood days. I remembered how efficiently my father wrung hens' necks and shouldn't have thought it, but found the memory uplifting.

As Jock neared his targets, one of them panicked into flight. Her navigational skills were so poor she flew with all the grace of a frozen turkey. It made it easy to catch her. I stuffed her into the box whilst the other, flustered without her pal, followed suit.

'Gotcha. You must be Dally. Join Dilly,' I said, and shut the lid.

Jock climbed down. 'Are they all right?' He peered through air holes punched into the box's side. 'They don't sound very happy.' He was definitely working on not repeating his last words. I wondered why. Maybe I'd find out on our way to Dingwall, if we ever got there.

I said, 'They'll be fine but I expect you know they'll need their wings clipped to stop their flying careers. Have you a sharp pair of scissors?' Momentarily I thought about the glinting, shining ones in Ann's nursing bag, but couldn't really justify using them. 'If not, we can get a pair in Dingwall. Come on, Jock. We'll miss the visiting time if we don't go now. Just put away your bike clips and mind and take those dratted long johns with you.'

Jock climbed into the car, carefully kicking his boots free of snow. Then he shut the door, sat back and sighed as if surrendering to an uncertain fate. Already he was making me feel nervous. Dingwall wasn't far away but my passenger with his eyes trained on the speedometer and whistling whenever it went over thirty mph had a slowing effect.

I don't know who was the most delighted when we got to the hospital but Jock's look of relief went as he got out.

'I'm thinking Willie's no keen to come home. Maybe having the telly'll do the trick.' He wiped his brow with the back of his hand. 'I wouldna like to think I got it for nothing. Anyhow, I'll no be watching it, watching—' He slapped his hand over his mouth.

'Uh! Willie says me always repeating myself drives him daft. It's just a habit I got into when I was on the road and keeping myself company but he says that's why he'd given up saying much to me,' Jock sounded plaintive. 'But how would I have known that if he wouldna tell me tell me?'

'I expect it's because he didn't want to hurt your feeling,' I said, moved at seeing Jock's hurt expression, 'but it sounds as if *he's* plenty to say to you these days. So that's good news and I'm sure he'll be delighted with the telly. Anyway, hospitals are always wanting their beds freed up so whether your brother likes it or not, he'll be home before he knows it.'

My confidence must have reassured Jock a little for he walked off quite jauntily whilst I went to find a parking place near a shoe shop.

I should have kept on my new boots. They wouldn't have been so obvious as the tell-tale shoebox I was now carrying.

'You're a long way from home.' Sister Shiach had come out of the chemist shop where I was now scissors-bound. She was laden with two large packs of incontinence pads. She swung them like weighing scales as she explained, 'These are for one of my thrifties. She thinks that drying her used ones saves money.' She rolled her eyes. 'I think her house smells like an ill-kept fish shop and *she* thinks I'm a representative of a spendthrift society.'

I didn't need to mention boots and maybe buying scissors to cut feathers wasn't a very good reason to be in Dingwall either so I explained about Jock and how he wanted to tempt Willie back home with a television. Hens, I considered, were surplus information.

'Sounds as if Willie's getting hospitalised. Silly blighter doesn't realise he's lucky having Jock.'

It's a funny world, I thought, remembering Raigmore and Miss

Caird, who'd had nobody. The last thing she'd have wanted was to be in hospital, but then she didn't have a caring brother chivvying her to get better and back home.

A wave of laughter and banter burst down the street, startling Sister Shiach. She looked at her watch. 'Heavens! That must be pub-closing time. I'll need to get on. You too.'

Then she bent her head and hissed, 'Blast! Look the other way. You'll never guess who's heading in this direction.'

15

PROGRESS OF A KIND

There was something heroic about Ginny Saunders-Hewitt. In a defiant stance against the weather she skittered towards us wearing impossibly high heels and a very short skirt. Maybe the fur jacket was keeping her warm or, more probably, it was where she and the Captain had just come from.

As soon as she caught sight of us, she grabbed her husband's arm. 'Oh, look! It's Sister Shiach and,' she aimed a cool if slightly ill-focused glance, 'her little helper!'

In a world of swirling snowflakes, the Captain's face was like a Belisha beacon of cheer. He stopped to button up his camelhair coat, a bit hindered by Ginny hanging on but still able to look about. He raised his eyebrows when he spotted a Morris Minor mounted halfway on the pavement and very near where we stood.

'So it is! If we'd spied that we'd have known it was you, Sister. Your parking skills are famous. Ha ha!'

Shortly after getting to know Sister Shiach, I'd learnt there was only one way to really annoy her, and the Captain's criticism of her driving had just done it. Blithely, he carried on. 'It's not something you do, is it? *You* just jolly stop.' His speech might not be as slurred as it had been at our last encounter, but I reckoned he must have lost some brain cells since then. He can't have known he was playing with fire.

Sister Shiach's eyes narrowed, her brow gathered, her lips tightened and she spread her feet as if readying for physical combat. For a delicious moment I thought she was about to clock the Captain with one of the incontinence bags but fortunately (or not) the car horn blasted.

'That's Jomo telling me not to hang about and that *we've* work to do. Nice to see *you*, Sister Macpherson, but don't you be standing outside too long in this weather. I don't want *you* to freeze.' And with that she hurried away.

'Whoops, I say! Must've touched a raw nerve there as well as stopping the good lady from getting on,' said the Captain, 'and maybe we should head home before we freeze too.' He nudged his wife and winked. 'And I'm sure that when we get there we'll think of a few ways to keep us warm, eh, Ginny Gin?'

'Oooh, Charles,' she giggled, 'You are a rascal. But come on. I never thought it'd be such fun revisiting those days of our youth. D'you think there'll be hot water for a bath as well?'

The pair staggered off in a waft of alcohol and mothballs, surely coming from the fur jacket. Maybe it too was enjoying a resurrection.

But this was no time for reflection. The hospital-visiting hour would soon be up and Jock had to be collected before I could finish Ann's list of patients. I'd make a quick nip to the chemist shop, then I'd be on my way.

'Good afternoon, Sister. Are you collecting someone's prescription? In this awful weather I suppose you'll be finding a lot of your patients are stuck at home, not able to collect them themselves.'

I wondered if the lady serving me was the pharmacist. Her grave manner, white coat and grey hair had the authority of someone used to giving advice. Behind the rimless spectacles was a shrewd gaze. I suspected that under it many a young chap bent on buying contraception would develop a sudden cough and go out of the shop with a packet of lozenges instead.

'Actually, I've come to buy a pair of good strong scissors,' I said.

'Oh, nobody's tablets then.' She sounded disappointed, but still eager to help, pointed to an array of cutting implements displayed in a glass cabinet. 'Would that be stitch, nail or plaster?'

I couldn't tell her she'd missed out on the feather category. 'Plaster, please.' I said, immediately regretting it when she came back with, 'Ah! Someone's broken limb healed now and ready for the cast to be cut off. Now who would that be?'

Thankfully, she immediately patted her mouth in a delicate way and looked about. 'Oh dear, that's confidential I suppose. It's just that we generally know every health matter around Dingwall. You'll understand it's only a kindly interest.' She leant over the counter and whispered, 'But Sister, you shouldn't have to buy scissors. Surely you're supplied with ones.'

I whispered back, 'Actually, I think I may have mislaid mine.'

It was worrying how easily the lie slipped out. I decided that the next time I came shopping I'd not be wearing the uniform even if I knew I was already marked. She'd clocked the shoe bag.

Nodding at them whilst wrapping up the scissors, she said, 'It's good you've had the time to get these. It must be your half-day but you're late for going off duty and I bet you'll be wanting to get home before the snow blocks the road. That plough's always late on the road. Have you far to go?' The question was casual, but I knew it was loaded.

It could have been fun not letting on but she'd such an interrogatory manner and I needed to be on my way that I relented and told her.

'Some of our Muir of Ord patients get their prescriptions elsewhere, you know,' she sounded annoyed, 'even if we give them a little advice for nothing. But you come back and see us again and if your patients can't collect their prescriptions, you be sure and get them here.'

'That Mabel Ross is awful nosy,' declared Jock once I'd collected him from the hospital and told him about the scissors. 'I was in school with her and she was as bad then – bigsy too. And the way she carries on you'd think she was the chemist and owned the place. I thought she was retired but she must be doing holiday relief for another assistant, assis —' He clamped down on the last word.

'That's strong stuff, Jock,' I said. 'I wonder what she'd have said if I told her the scissors were for cutting your hens' feathers.'

But Jock was too busy watching the snowplough clearing the road before us to respond. Eventually he clucked in a disapproving way, reminiscent of Dilly and Dally, 'Oh I mind when we cleared the road just with shovels. That's awful heavy machinery they're using. And see the mannies shovelling out that sand? I bet there's stones in it. They'll grind down under pressure of the snow so when it goes we'll be left in a right mess. You can get a bad bike accident if you hit a pothole.'

I wondered what was making Jock so scratchy. He'd told me that Willie was getting home in a couple of days so he should have looked happier. Instead he kept playing his fingers over his knee and whistling softly and tunelessly.

As I drew up at his house, I said, 'You'll be looking forward to a bit of telly tonight. It makes good company.'

There was a momentary silence, then Jock burst out, 'I'll no be switching it on. Willie's been telling me what he's been watching watching. Mannies wrestling, Nursie, wrestling!' He shook his head in disbelief and blew his nose with a scrap of material, last used, I suspected, to clean his bike. 'I wouldna want mannies like that in our house, house.'

At this rate I was never going to get back to Muir of Ord, but

101

Jock was looking so upset I went for an exasperated, 'Och, Jock! The only mannies likely to be in your house are the two of you and sometimes I'm thinking that's two too many. Come on, I'll show you how to work that telly so you get a decent programme and we'll get Dilly and Dally sorted before they make the great escape.' I added hopefully. 'It shouldn't take long.'

Would Sister Shiach be proud of me, I wondered. It was nearly five o'clock and I'd left someone in her district happily dividing his attention between responding to a TV panel game quiz and chatting to Dilly and Dally through the box holes. 'Now, hennies, stop complaining. At least you're inside, but as soon as you get to know the others, you can join them. I'm sorry we had to clip your wings, but Nursie says you'll soon love being stay-at-home girls.'

He'd not be used to getting any kind of response so I wondered how he and Willie would get on once he was discharged. He seemed to have emerged fighting fit, in every sense of the word.

It was a pity that the same didn't apply to Miss Forbes. After I finished Ann's list and before going back to her house, I thought I should check on the old lady. Since she wouldn't welcome a random visit, I needed an excuse to call. I knew I had one as soon as I saw there was neither a light showing in her window nor smoke coming out of the chimney.

16

DOG CONTROL

'It's all right, LBP,' I called, going into the house a lot more carefully than the last time. 'It's only me.'

There was no answering sabre-rattling growl, which, in a way, was worrying. I couldn't find the hallway light and had to grope made my way to the living room where the sound came of someone troubled for air. I made to switch on the light but was stopped as Miss Forbes wheezed, 'Don't you dare put on that light. LBP and I are enjoying a little peace and quiet in the dark. Can't you see that?'

'No!' I said, and banged down the switch.

At least LBP wasn't a problem. In fact, she'd become a pathetic-looking little bundle shivering at her mistress's feet. Now, shiny with retained fluid, they were even more swollen than ever, with the same oedema stretching up her legs. Heaven help her if they got knocked. A skin under such pressure would easily break, allowing serous fluid to leak out, making a soggy route for sores and ulcers to follow. It was a bleak prospect.

I wished I'd spoken to her GP earlier. My patient needed constant care that would really get rid of the fluid, take the pressure off her lungs and heart and get her legs back in working order.

She flapped a tired hand. 'Just give me a mo' and I'll be all right.'

Apart from discussing the joy of straight guy ropes and reef knots, I knew there was only one way to my patient's troubled heart.

'Look! I know you're worried about your doggy, but really you're doing her no favours at the moment. You don't want to get to the stage where you really can't look after her, now do you?'

Making a sudden decision, I got down on my hunkers and gave LBP straight talk. 'Now that we're good pals, I'm happy to take you home with me. Then your mistress can concentrate on getting herself better and she'll do that quicker if she's in hospital.'

Miss Forbes struggled to reach down to fondle the dog's ears, seemingly unaware they were flattened, or that LBP was showing me bared teeth. Even if the bonding signs between us weren't favourable, I persevered. 'And, LBP, you'll be good company for me, but I'll need to phone the doctor first. See what he says.'

Miss Forbes made a long and gusty sigh, then nodded, 'His number's in the telephone's wee pull-out drawer.'

The doctor answered at the first ring. He sounded wearied. 'Uh! Miss Forbes. My old soldier. I worry about her, especially as I'm not sure what I can do. She messes about with her medication so consistently knows best. What she actually needs, of course, is to go into hospital to get properly sorted.' There was a pause. 'But I bet she won't.'

'I think she might now,' I ventured, 'I've a feeling that she knows that staying where she is at the moment isn't an option.'

'Really? That's good and if that's the case, I'll phone for an ambulance. I'll leave it up to you to decide if you need to go with her.' The phone crashed down.

Miss Forbes might not be particularly operational, but she'd got herself out of her chair and was able between wheezes to give some directions. 'Right, Sister, you might have to fight your way into my bedroom but you'll find a suitcase on top of the wardrobe.

It's packed already. Be Prepared, as you know, is the only way.' She bent down and spoke to LBP. 'And you'll have to be a good dog and do what your temporary boss tells you. She's not as grim as she looks.'

There surely couldn't be any bigger compliment than being trusted with LBP, but as I located the case, I worried about Miss Forbes's level of faith. A dog that wasn't used to anybody other than its owner might not settle for a new minder, especially this one. And in the meantime, what would I do if I'd to go in the ambulance? The house was cold and LBP looked so small, miserable and frightened, it was going to be difficult leaving her here on her own.

Miss Forbes must have been reading my mind. She said, 'I don't want you coming with me. I'll be fine as long as I know my dog's all right.' The set of her jaw made argument impossible. After realigning her hairnet, she fumbled in her pocket and produced a lipstick. Aiming it at her lips, she drew a bright red gash. 'There!' A smile tugged at the corner of her mouth. 'I'm all set and there's the ambulance. After you've taken out my case, you go back and lock up.'

'You'll find LBP's basket in the kitchen,' Miss Forbes had instructed. 'She hasn't been using it much lately.' She'd grimaced. 'Not good, I know, but she's been more of a comfort than a hot water bottle.'

I presumed she meant the basket that was so well chewed only half of it remained, so I carried it as carefully to the car as I did LBP. I tried to tempt her with some food when we were back in Ann's house but, child-like, she set her head away from it.

I'd tied her fringe back with an elastic band. Maybe that had been a mistake because now I couldn't help but see her eyes brimming with sadness and fear. Touched by such abject misery, I took her into my bedroom and that was the second blunder.

When I woke next day, the little room with its sweetie-pink walls, matching carpet, rose-sprigged bedding and curtains had become Halitosis Hall. LBP's basket too showed even more signs of deterioration, and her eyes watched beadily over an edge lowered practically to the ground

'You'll need to see a dentist,' I said, jumping out of bed, 'and Ann's going to be furious what with her black bag being slavered over and her house smelling like a fish factory.'

I shoved up the bedroom window and let in a blast of air. Before, Ann's garden had been pristine under its mantle of white, but now it had small yellow patches on it made by LBP last night. I supposed I should be grateful that she knew better than to pee inside.

I bent down and patted her. 'If I didn't know you better I'd say you were trying to look personable. Come on, you've something to do before we go to work. Ann's snow needs some more melting.'

'We couldn't help noticing the ambulance at Miss Forbes's house.' Mrs Munro, dishtowel in hand, met me at the car. Her eyes, alive with concern and curiosity, suddenly took in LBP. Her face lit up.

'What a cute wee doggie,' she cried. 'You didn't say you had one.'

'Mind your manners, LBP,' I urged, worried that Mrs Munro's twiddling fingers reaching through the small space left at the top of the car window might get bitten off. I got out of the car.

LBP showed the whites of her eyes then bent her head as if in despair. Already her foetid breath was misting the car windscreen. I shouldn't have had porridge for breakfast. I could feel it turning in my stomach.

'Och, Nurse, is that a rubber band she's got in her hair?' Mrs Munro scolded. 'The poor wee thing'll no like that. Could we take her in to see Himself, d'you think? He loves dogs – is always on about having one, and to tell you the truth,' she dropped her voice and looked around as if the whole of Muir of Ord could hear, 'I think she might be the very one to brighten him up. Thought I'd catch you and mention it before you go in. Maybe it's the diabetes and maybe it's being retired with little to do, but he gets down particularly at this time of year.'

'He'll want to run a mile from this one,' I pulled a face. 'She's a smelly wee warrior and needs a bath and a visit to the hair dresser *and* she'll make your house smell like the glue works.'

Mrs Munro had the brightening look of someone on a happy-making mission. 'D'you think that living in a croft was nothing but fresh air? Come on! I'm dying to take her in.' Already she'd opened the car door and with only a cursory glance in my direction, lifted out LBP before I could scream, 'She might bite!'

But all LBP did was wag a tail I'd only ever seen tucked between her legs. She gazed trustingly up at Mrs Munro, who tucked her under arm and patted her head. This met with LBP's full approval.

'Rubber band! What's the nurse thinking of?' There was real rebuke in Mrs Munro's voice as she headed back into the house. LBP cocked her ears and looked as if this was the first time since last night she'd heard anything sensible.

'Is LBP all right?'

I knew it would be the first thing Miss Forbes would ask. Driving in to Inverness, I'd been wondering what I'd tell her. Now, sitting during the afternoon visiting hours in a ward where I'd so recently worked, I still wasn't sure. For a moment, I glanced round the ward.

Sister Gall's influence was fading. Had she still been here, I knew that she'd have been bursting into the rooms like a bad fairy breaking up a party. Visitors found sitting on beds would have been sent packing and doubtless a grape count would be held at the end of the visiting hour.

It was good to be in a ward that felt so much more relaxed, and I hoped that if the new sister was on duty, she was having a nice cup of tea in her office. Still, it seemed sinful doing nothing. Sister Gall might have been small but she'd left such a long shadow I'd to resist popping into the sluice for an inventory check.

As soon as she'd asked about her dog, Miss Forbes put her oxygen mask back on again. She was still breathless and needed a load of pillows and a hospital backrest to help her to sit up. Her hand fluttered over her winceyette nightdress, checking its Peter Pan collar lay flat. Not so controllable was the pink lace of her bri-nylon bed jacket rippling a distress message over her ample bosom.

'LBP is just tickety-boo,' I said. 'Never better. You mustn't worry about her. She's settling down beautifully.'

And so she was. But in the Munros' house.

'Och, but is she no the bonniest thing,' Mr Munro had cried and patted his lap onto which LBP, jettisoning her little old lady persona, had immediately sprung. 'See! She's made herself at home. But what's this?' He pointed to the matted hair with a look of disapproval.

'It's like this,' I began.

In hospital now and recalling the conversation, I knew I'd have to settle for the truth. 'Miss Forbes, d'you know the Munros? They live quite near you?'

She nodded and managed, 'Couple. Retired, I believe. Nice.' Through the mask, she sounded as if she was under water.

I took a deep breath. 'They also love animals and miss them as much as the croft life they left. Now Mr Munro's driving his wife bananas, being an under-occupied man in the house, you know . . .' Encouraged by Miss Forbes's faint smile, I hurried on, 'They're keen to look after LBP. It'll be a great way for Mr Munro to get out from under his wife's feet as well as get some exercise himself. Now I know you trusted me with her, but to tell you the truth, the Munros will have more time and LBP's bound to give them a new interest.' I waited anxiously for a response.

'Okay. That's okay.' She leant back on the pillows. 'Sounds like it's ideal and if anything happens . . .' her voice tailed off.

I leant over and whispered, 'Just do what the doctors tell you and you'll soon be back home cracking the whip, but in the meantime you can be sure she'll be as well cared for as you obviously are.'

17

RESCUE PACKAGE

So that I could visit Miss Forbes, I'd asked Sister Shiach to cover for me. Now I was phoning to let her know that I was back on duty.

She must have picked up on my anxiety about my patient and the possibility of an orphan dog because she said, 'Look, you know what a bit of routine care, kindness and regular medication can do. I'm pretty sure Miss Forbes will soon be home and back to driving Ann up the wall, with LBP helping.' She chuckled. 'What is it about you, anyway? It's never straightforward stuff, is it? Have you ever considered the simple joy of giving an enema? No! Don't bother answering.' She hurried on. 'I'm not complaining, just observing. Anyway, you'll be pleased to know that Willie's been discharged from hospital. I went to check that he and Jock were all right and what do you think I found?'

'Willie doing a Cordon Bleu cookery course?'

'Ha! No, you silly chump! They've got a pair of hens who've moved in. Jock says the other ones don't like them so they're keeping Dilly and Dally inside until he makes a house for them. I don't think he should bother. They seemed perfectly at home where they are.'

'In their box?'

'No! Perched on the back of the boys' chairs.' In a throwaway line, she added, 'God help them if the sanny-manny calls.'

'You can only mean the sanitary inspector.'

'Yes. If he does visit the boys and starts complaining about their unconventional approach to domesticity, I'll phone and tell him they're all orphans and ask where's his caring heart.'

I was cheered by the chat. 'But what did Willie think of Dilly and Dally? I bet they were a surprise.'

'Actually, he was too busy arguing with Jock about what telly programme to watch to think much about a couple of hens making themselves so at home. I'd never heard him so vocal. You wouldn't think a trip outside four walls would change somebody so.'

'Let's hope the same applies to Miss Forbes,' I said, putting down the phone and going to check up on LBP and her minders.

'So that's you back, and how's the patient? She'd have been pleased to see you. By Jove, yes.' Mrs Munro had answered the door. She had a ball of brightly coloured wool under her arm and a length of striped knitting in her hand. She nodded at it. 'And look! You've caught me relaxing. With Himself out giving the doggy a walk, I thought I'd have a minute to myself otherwise that poor black bairn in Africa will be past needing his jersey.'

'It's early days for Miss Forbes,' I said, 'but I know a wee dog who's landed on her feet. Her mum was really happy when I told her you were looking after her. Half her cure, I'd say but,' I felt obliged to ask, 'are you sure that having LBP isn't a bother?'

'What?' Mrs Munro almost screamed. 'It's a pleasure. I haven't seen Angus so happy for yonks. He's out walking her at the moment. We think that a wee stroll on hard ground'll help wear down her nails.' She nudged me with her unoccupied elbow, mischief in her eyes. 'And maybe it'll help pare down Angus's ones too. I'm always on at him to take exercise but he says that after a lifetime of walking after sheep, he feels daft doing it on his own.'

I joined in her laughter then felt a little ashamed when I saw

Mr Munro coming towards us, looking so happy, a smile lit his craggy face. 'Look who's here,' he said to LBP who, snuggled under his jacket, looked out from the top of it with the superior gaze of a grandstand spectator. The rubber band had gone and she now had a short fringe, which made her look like the good girl of the class.

Mr Munro explained, 'I'm carrying her because she might be feeling the cold so soon after we'd bathed her and given her that wee haircut. Of course we'd to cut yon felt patches off her coat too.' He patted the dog's head proudly. 'She was better behaved than any sheep being clipped.' For a moment, he looked anxious. 'You don't think Miss Forbes will mind, do you, Sister?'

'Apart from the fact that she might not recognise her, I think she'll be delighted.'

'We've been round to Rose Cottage,' Mr Munro continued. 'We thought we should check everything's in order, didn't we, LBP?' He bent his head and she licked his nose enthusiastically. 'I was thinking that the front gate needed fixing. I'm quite handy, you know.' Turning up the palms of his hands, he spat on them then rubbed them together as if readying for work.

'Angus!' scolded his wife, 'that's so unhygienic. What will Sister be thinking?'

'I'm thinking Miss Forbes will thank her lucky stars she's got such good neighbours. And would you be thinking of visiting her yourselves?'

Mrs Munro was eager. 'My! Yes! Surely! That's a good idea! You know, when I was in at the post office I was telling the folk there that she'd been taken into Raigmore and, of course, you know what wee shops are like. Word's got out and now everybody's anxious to hear how she is. She's so well thought of in the village but herself being so private and proud.' Marking her respect for that, Mrs Munro put her hand to her mouth to muffle her voice.

'Folk don't like her to think they're prying. But surely she won't mind Angus and me calling, especially if she knows we've got LBP.'

'I bet she'd love a visit, but maybe give her a day or two,' I said.

As the Munros went inside and I turned for home, there came a sound like a creaking gate but from high above. I concentrated hard, wondering what it could be. Listening, I eventually realised that it was a lone goose calling for its fellow travellers. It sounded so forlorn that despite myself I made the connection. I too would miss my companion, even if she was smelly and had only been with me for one night.

By the end of the week, the snow was clearing and the LBP bouquet removed from the house in time for Ann coming back. She'd phoned to say that her mother was recovering. The same could be said for Miss Forbes, if to a lesser degree.

'Himself and I went to see her yesterday,' Mrs Munro had reported. 'She says she's feeling so much better she should be home, but the ward sister says she's going nowhere until she accepts having a home help.'

'Aye. That sister's mebbe not the old school, but she's fly enough to sort out her patients without them noticing,' put in Mr Munro. 'A bit like your injection, Sister. I never felt a thing.'

To my surprise, he'd been watching the needle go in. So was LBP, who sat at his feet, baring her teeth.

'Crikey, that's clean pearlies,' I said, meanwhile stepping out of their range. 'LBP could be leading a gleam team.'

'Chewing on a butcher's bone did that,' Mrs Munro explained with a fond smile. 'And once I knit a wee jacket for her, Angus'll be able to give her a proper walk and that'll really sort out her nails.'

The old man stood up, seeming full of purpose. 'You know, Sister,' he said, in his considering way, 'I was thinking you don't really have to be too smart to give injections.'

'No?'

Mrs Munro, shocked, turned from cleaning the sink tap. 'Angus!'

'Well, *you* could easy do it. I mean, you've served your apprenticeship. I never heard one sheep complaining. And it would mean the nurses can get on with looking after other folk.' Then, as if producing his killer line, he added, 'And we wouldn't be always anxious in case they slept in.'

I could have protested, but he had a point so I said, 'What a great idea. It would give you far more independence and I reckon you'd be great at it, Mrs Munro. You keep everything so spotlessly clean and must have watched often enough. I bet you've thought to yourself you could do it, and far better too.'

She stepped back to admire the taps and bit her lip. 'I suppose I could have a try, but I'd need to be watched, for the first whiley anyway.'

'It's a deal. Now, have you any messages for Miss Forbes? I'm planning to visit her this evening.'

Mr Munro reached for his cap. 'Would you tell her I'm making that thing she calls a cat flap on her backdoor? We spoke about it when we visited her. It'll be handy for LBP and now that I've fixed the front gate she'll get the run of the whole garden. It'll be grand if I can get it done before she gets home.'

Strangely, when I got to her bedside, it wasn't Miss Forbes's first topic of conversation. She looked better and was managing without the help of oxygen. Her lipstick had hit the right target and the hairnet was realigned. Still, she looked despondent.

'You know,' she said, looking round the place, 'I've had a full life. I've been round the world with the guiding movement and had many an adventure on the way. So I've been fortunate. Lucky too for living in Muir of Ord. I didn't realise so many people knew me or cared.' She pointed to a pile of cards stacked on her locker.

'But I've been guilty of shutting myself away. I've always been a coper and in charge of others, so it's been hard for me to acknowledge I've needed help.' Her voice trailed away as she fiddled with the buzzer's cable.

'I bet you'll be surprised at how much better things will be for you back at home,' I said. 'It's easy to get in a muddle when you're feeling poorly, but if you've a home help, I'm sure she'll help you get things on an even keel.'

I'd been careful what I'd said but Miss Forbes went on as if she hadn't heard. 'I used to think it'd be easier having a tinker's life, not bothered by possessions and able to travel the freeways of life.' She looked about her as if to check whether anybody was listening, then leant towards me. 'But yesterday a patient was admitted. I was only heading for the toilet, otherwise I might not have seen her. I didn't want to gawp but I couldn't help but notice her. She had such beautiful bright red hair.'

I noted the past tense.

Miss Forbes continued, 'A sharp-voiced woman came in with her, along with a couple of ambulance men. My! But she was loud for the size of her.' Miss Forbes smiled as if paying tribute to a fellow foghorn. 'Anyway, she said she'd found the girl slumped in a close, off the High Street. People weren't paying any attention to her, thought she was a drunk, but this woman said she knew her and that any fool could see that she'd taken a fit.'

'So she raised the alarm?'

'She certainly did that. I don't know who she was but she seemed to know her way about the place. Said the girl needed to go into the room opposite the office and get immediate attention.'

A burst of laughter came from the people visiting the patient in the bed next to Miss Forbes. It seemed to mock her evident sadness. She shrugged and gazed at a ward window, its flimsy curtains barely concealing a black night.

'You know, Sister, I rather think that poor girl didn't survive. Soon after she was admitted, a man with red curly hair came in. He must've been a relation. He sounded terribly upset. In the end there was such a lot of shouting the sharp-voiced woman led him away.' Her voice trembled as she continued, 'Soon after that, the girl went somewhere else too. It was after men came with something that sounded like a metal container on wheels. They must've taken her away. The sound of that thing was dreadful.' She buried her face in her hands.

If I'd still been working here I supposed I'd have been so busy dealing with a patient's death I might not have considered how it could affect others in the ward. Now, as a visitor, I saw such distress and the words stuck in my throat. All I could do was acknowledge Miss Forbes's tears. Fishing around in her camel-coloured dressing gown hanging by the bedside, I found a man-sized hanky and handed it to her.

I thought about Dusty. It had to be her. I wondered how her brother would cope without her and where was he when she needed him most.

Later, I left Miss Forbes, now recovered enough to consider she had a future, and with a home help, a better one at that. As I drove out of Inverness I saw a group of men making for the brash lighting of a pub near Inverness's harbour. They had someone familiar-looking with them. I figured they were supporting him in the best way they knew.

As for me, rosemary bushes might not grow wild or freely in the North of Scotland, but they do in other places and whenever I see one, I remember Miss Caird and Dusty and see their similarity.

18

A VISIT TO EASTER ROSS

With her mother better, Ann had returned and we were having a work-handover chat in her office. As she realigned a bottle of Savlon on its shelf, she sounded relaxed. 'Well! You know you've practically put me out of a job. I used to worry how I'd fit in caring for anybody else needing as much attention as Miss Forbes and Mr Munro.'

'They'll still be delighted to see you,' I said, 'if only to show that they can manage with a little less input. Mind you, they're both pretty busy. If Miss Forbes isn't organising her home help she's discussing garden improvements with Mr Munro.'

'And what about LBP?' Ann was dubious.

'She's looking great, apart from the candy-striped coat Mrs Munro knitted for her.' I grimaced. 'But at least she only has it on for walks. The Munros are giving her regular ones and that's helping keep her nails down as well.'

I glanced over at the clinic's shelving, hoping I'd put everything other than the Savlon in its accustomed place. Ann's black bag, now minus LBP's attentions, was nearly back to its former glory but she might find that the heavy-duty nail clippers stored inside were suffering from metal fatigue.

I took them out and showed them to her. 'Look, Ann, I'm sorry, but these'll need sharpening. Maybe instead of cutting their toenails I should have had your patients taking walks instead. I know you wanted me to help them bath but they wouldn't allow me to do anything else.'

'Hey! That's all right!' she protested. 'Nobody's going to die for the lack of a bath.'

'They all took one look at me and decided that they were fine apart from their nails.' I cast my eyes heavenwards. 'Since then, word must have got out because I've had a load of folk wanting them done. Nail-clipper par excellence, that's me!'

Ann was kind. 'Ah, but you'll have helped them to move easier as well as saved their sock toes from getting holes.' She giggled. 'Anyway, your secret's safe. You're telling me that you're off to Fearn. It's about twenty miles away so I'm sure that's far enough away for a rumour to get lost. That's Flora's district – where's she off to?'

I thought about the nurse I was to replace and explained that she was going on a childcare course. I added, 'It starts on Monday. I'm having a few days off before, then I'll go over on Sunday.'

'I think the folk in Easter Ross take their Sabbaths seriously.' Ann was wry. 'The most they use their cars then is for taking them to church. If I was you, I'd avoid arriving when the service is over and the folk come out.'

Driving on a Sunday had its advantages. The road was almost traffic-free, but with lots of cars parked outside churches. It made driving through Evanton, Alness and Invergordon quick, and in the absence of snow, easy. I glanced at my watch. At this rate I was going to arrive early. Maybe I should slow down, admire the scenery, take my time.

Towards the west, snow-covered mountains dominated the skyline, whilst I was heading towards flat, fertile countryside stretching in a plain towards the east. There weren't many trees on this route, but in my imagination I read weird alphabets formed by the bare-leaved branches of ash trees against a pale February sky. I fancied they told indecipherable tales borne and shaped by a rogue Siberian wind. In the distance, there were grey glimpses of a hungry sea, its bite marks showing in the uneven-looking coastline.

I drove past occasional lines of cars on the road where drivers had run out of church parking spaces. I was surprised there were so many places of worship and all so austere in design they looked like grim sentries catering for a congregation that liked its religion neat. This, however, might not be the case in Fearn where its Abbey name spoke of pre-Reformation times. I'd missed the turn-off to the village, and taken the Balintore road instead. Hardly a minute later, I saw a Fearn Abbey sign pointing to a church on the opposite side a little way off the road.

I slowed down to admire the leaded windows set in weathered stone of a very old building. It wore the mellow look of somewhere which had survived far worse times than today, but the same couldn't be said about my driving.

I realised that I'd just passed Fearn and would need to turn back. This allowed the faithful flocking out of church a wondrous sight of someone doing a very bad three-point turn.

'Och well, it could have been worse. You could've run over some of the congregation,' said Flora, reacting to my bad driving and timing tale. 'Just come away in and forget it. It'll only be the talk of the village until there's something more interesting to speak about. Anyway, I've been telling my patients to expect a replacement.' She added with a twinkle, 'With my house stuck right in the middle of the village, everybody'll have seen your car parked outside it so they'll already know who you are and that you're strange.' She chuckled mightily. 'To the area, I mean! Come on, you must be hungry.'

We sat at a table set out with a cold-meat salad. 'I'm sorry it's such plain fare but I wasn't sure when you'd be,' she said, and bent her head.

Too late, I realised that she was saying grace. Blushing, I put down my fork.

With a mischievous look, Flora lifted hers. 'It's a proper Christian act to come so early. It means I can get on the road before dark.' She chewed on an egg so hardboiled it had black bits round the yolk. What would Dr Duncan say to that, I wondered.

Swallowing hard, Flora continued, 'Miss Macleod's great at sending us off on courses and I'm looking forward to going to Aberdeen. You always meet nice folk and as much as I love district nursing, it can be lonely working on your own. You know, even if the doctor runs his surgery from his house in the village, I'm more likely to hear from him than see him.' She grimaced. 'Sometimes I think we operate on parallel universes. Thanks to the bally answering machine, he can leave any old message for me but if I need to get back to him, it's most likely he'll be out on his rounds so it's his poor wife who's got to deal with my call.'

She finished her meal then shot up from her chair. 'Now if it's okay with you, I'll give you a quick run through the work and then I'll go. You'll then get a chance to have a look around the village in the daylight and get your bearings. Look! I've got a map for you as well. It'll show you the area I cover.'

When Flora left, the house felt empty. I was rather glad I was only covering for her district for a short period. Her patients mightn't have the time to lament the absence of such a bright, friendly, energetic presence. I walked round the village wondering where all the people who'd come out of church had gone. The place seemed deserted. Only the odd curtain twitch and smoking chimney let me know that there was life behind the closed doors.

A modest little stone marking Fearn as the birthplace of Peter

Fraser was more informative. It said he'd become prime minister in New Zealand from 1940 to 1949. How remarkable! In terms of history, I reckoned there must be someone here who knew either him or of him and how he'd made such an epic journey. But I wouldn't find that out today so I returned to the house and spent a more profitable few hours poring over Flora's map.

When the phone rang in the middle of the night, I was glad I had.

19

FOG AND ICE

The speaker on the phone sounded far too brisk for such a late call. 'Doctor here. I'm sorry to call you but Mrs Vass has gone into labour. She's not due for a week but she's just rung and told me.'

'Mrs Vatt?' I could only mumble.

There was a brief silence, then with a forced laugh, the caller continued, 'Ah! Flora's relief. I'd forgotten she was away this week. Sorry, you must think this is a rude awakening, but you see the reason I'm calling is that Mrs *Vass* has such a history of quick labours she'll need a nurse to go with her in the ambulance to Raigmore. I suppose you'll not have had the time to find out where Balintore is yet?' He began to sound anxious.

'Actually, I have. It's on the map Flora's given me,' I said, wanting to give a good account of myself and neglecting to say I'd nearly arrived there by mistake. 'It's only a couple of the miles down the road that takes you past the Abbey, isn't it?'

'Yup. Not actually quite as far as that. The Vasses' farm's just on Balintore's outskirts. You'll easily find it.' He gave a brief chuckle. 'I don't suppose there's too many lights on at two in the morning. Anyway, I've called Charlie, the ambulance driver, and he's likely to be there before you, so look out for him.'

'How old is she and which pregnancy is this for her?'

'She's an elderly multip – fourth kid. She's pretty unflappable and she should be fine, but take your delivery equipment with you anyway. I'm sure you'll get there before anything happens and we'll maybe catch up in the morning, eh?' Without bothering for a response, he rang off.

Blast! I was so dopy with sleep I hadn't even asked what the name of the farm was. I hoped the doctor was right about the lights and that Balintore wouldn't complicate his directions with a flood-lit barn dance.

Piling into my uniform, I raced into Flora's office, grabbed a delivery pack and stumbled out into the night.

Then I stopped, shocked. Clearly the doctor hadn't looked out of the window, and neither had I. There was nothing but grey mist enveloping everywhere outside in a thick freezing fog. There wasn't a breath of wind. Nothing moved. Time stood still. Silence. There were gravel chips surrounding the house, handy, Flora had said, for letting the village folk know she had visitors calling. Now as I stepped on those tell-tale stones, they merely muttered as if in disapproval that anybody was out and disturbing their peace.

The fog chilled by stealth. It was marginally warmer in the car but with a gathering sense of panic I saw that the ice-crazed windscreen had killed visibility. I got out of the car and in a state of fuddled anxiety breathed, then scrubbed over the screen. At some point later I might marvel that hyperventilation can thaw out frozen glass to make a vision porthole. Right now, I was just grateful it did the job.

I shot back into the car. 'Right. Let's go!' I said, turning the key. The car engine coughed into life. At least something was alive in this frozen planet.

Thanks to the map, I didn't take the wrong road otherwise I could have landed back in Muir of Ord or Tain to the North. I was sure I was making for Fearn Abbey, less so when the car

123

wheels fell silent and went where they wanted. My heart thumped. Would I ever get the hang of driving on ice?

'Turn your steering wheel into the direction of a skid,' Sister Shaich had advised. 'And going slowly's better than braking.'

I was never completely convinced by her motoring advice. Anyway, she wasn't referring to a situation where the midwife's late arrival could mean a baby's early one but in an ambulance. I accelerated. The fog pressed in. The car waltzed sideways. It was so near the verge it nearly hit the just visible Abbey sign, but at least I knew I was on the right road.

I drove at a crawling speed, aiming, hopefully, for the middle of the road. I was beginning to think that this nightmare would never end when I saw at last tail-lights seeing off the mist in a triumphant arc of red.

It had to be the ambulance. I made for it.

I drew up, wound down the car window and spoke to the ambulance driver looming out of the mist.

'Charlie?'

'Aye, by name and a right one by nature.' He was young with an open, sunny face slightly at odds with his rockabilly hairstyle. 'We were beginning to think we'd have to send out a search party,' he said. 'I've already got Mrs Vass on board so as soon as you park your car we can go.' He rubbed his hands. Maybe he was pleased to see me, or maybe it was because of the biting cold. 'Delivering a patient to hospital's one thing, but I'm not so keen on one being delivered here,' he jerked his head at the ambulance. 'Mind you, there was one last week . . .'

But I was too busy getting rid of the car that I didn't wait to hear the rest. Anxious to get on the road, I raced back, but a large blue-dungaree-clad backside reversing out of the back of the ambulance blocked the entrance.

'Ach, Jimmy, mind out – there's someone behind you.' It must be my patient, talking to her husband with affectionate exasperation, 'And for goodness' sake, don't stand on her.'

I moved quickly, avoiding the big feet of a huge man stepping down from the ambulance. As he straightened up, he looked down at me in surprise then promptly shouted into the ambulance, 'Och, Meg, it's not the usual nurse and it's a terrible night. Nobody sensible would be out in it. Why don't I take you in the car? It'd be quicker and *she*,' he nodded in my direction, 'could look after the bairns.' He paused, then added reflectively, 'Even if they are a handful.'

The reply was swift. 'First I've heard you say that. Anyway, don't be daft, I told you Flora was away this week and of course you didn't listen. You never do, but you're right. It is perishing. Go on inside. You'll need to get your sleep if you want to get the bairns up for school, and *stop* fussing. I'm sure I'm in good hands. Anyway, the last time you came with me to hospital you fainted.'

I passed the man, climbed into the ambulance and tried for a reassuring, 'She's going to be fine. We'll take good care of her. It's great you're at home and she doesn't have to worry about the family.'

He looked at me through thick National Health spectacles. 'I wouldna be too sure of that,' he said morosely and slammed the door shut.

As soon as he did, Meg moved from her sitting-up position to slide down under some blankets to make herself as comfortable as you could on a stretcher-covered couch, offering all the comfort of a park bench.

'Thank goodness he's gone,' she said. 'Honestly, that man of mine makes such a fuss he makes everyone round him nervous. I hope he didn't offend you?'

I explained how I was only here for a week but already had managed to fit in an ambulance trip at a godforsaken hour in the middle of the night in thick fog, and all at the back of beyond. 'And loving every minute of it,' I concluded.

She laughed. 'You could be like me and be in labour as well.'

'Well, if I was I don't think I'd be half as calm, but let's see how things are before we get on the road.'

Her contractions, even if they were quite strong, weren't bothering her, and the baby's heartbeat sounded regular and strong. Neither the claustrophobic setting of the ambulance nor the weather conditions nor her own had affected her blood pressure. It was probably more normal than mine.

'Right?' called Charlie, then without bothering for a reply, he started the engine. It gave a full-throttle roar.

'Well if the kids weren't awake before, they'll certainly will be now,' said Meg with a mischievous glint in her eye.

The ambulance shot forward.

'Fancy swapping places?' I asked, thrown into the opposite couch.

'Certainly not. To tell you the truth, I'm looking forward to getting my feet up in Raigmore. Labour's never been a problem to me – there's far more of that at home.' She stretched work-coarsened hands before her and twiddled her fingers. 'I can't understand patients wanting an early discharge. Now they must have an easy life of it.'

She looked so calm that if I hadn't felt her abdomen tightening to show she really was having contractions I might have thought she wasn't in labour, a sentiment she shared, as she mused, 'I hope I'm not a fraud, they're only wee niggles but we thought it best to call the doctor and he said that I should get to Raigmore what with it being two hours of a journey from here.'

'But maybe longer with this fog,' called Charlie in full happy mode. The ambulance slid a little to the right. 'Whoops. Icy! Did you feel that?'

'No,' I lied, striving to put mind over matter. Perhaps my stomach was heaving because we'd just skidded. I might have left those childhood Nairn-to-Dingwall journeys behind, but travel sickness still dogged me. The twisting road didn't help and ambulance seating meant I was facing my patient, a position as conducive to nausea as those bus petrol and fag fumes of my past had been.

'Take deep breaths,' someone advised, or was I confusing that with women in labour? If I tried controlled and deep breathing it might alarm Meg, but she seemed to have fallen asleep so I had a go. Risking a cricked neck, I turned my head so that I could look in the same direction as Charlie.

He was going carefully and I supposed he was so familiar with the road he could cope with a windscreen that looked as if it had been smeared with Vaseline. It made the everyday shapes of bushes, trees, farms and homes look so dream-like it could have put you in a trance-like state, if you were a good traveller.

Deep breaths, I said to myself. Hang on. Look straight ahead.

Meg began to stir, then sat up and started foraging around.

'Getting sore?' I asked, stopping breathing.

She tidied her slightly greying hair behind her ears in an absent-minded way and flashed such a brilliant smile you might have thought she was going on holiday. 'No. I'm trying to find my knitting.' Her voice was calm. 'I don't want to bother you, but I think it must be in the suitcase. Could you have a look?'

She was as pink-cheeked in her exertions as I feared I was a growing green. Any minute now, I thought, as another queasy wave engulfed me, she'll suggest we should swap places. If she did, I might take her up on the offer.

Instead I said, 'I'll get it. No bother.' I knelt down. If I look down for just a second, I thought, I really will be sick, and in this bloomin' suitcase. By luck and blindly fishing around in it I came upon a bag with knitting needles and wool.

'Keeping your options open?' I asked, handing it over and noting that the Paton and Baldwin's wool was yellow.

'Uh huh.' For a moment she looked at me in a considering way. 'I'm not a gambler, but I bet it's a boy. We've three already. Jimmy would like a girl, but I'm not fussy. As long as it's all right.' She swung into action with her needles. 'If this journey's long enough I'll maybe get this matinee jacket finished.'

Instead of upping the drama of being heavily pregnant in a vehicle sliding all over the place, Meg was concentrating on her knitting. She was amazing. How could I tell her her midwife was so weedy?

I sneaked a sickness bowl hanging cup-like from a hook fixed to a shelf above me. I hoped she hadn't noticed. The feel of chrome was as cold in my hand as the sweat gathering on my brow but at last we cleared the smaller roads and reached the comparative straightness of the A9. We were almost at Alness and the driver was speeding up. Even if the streetlights still wore halos of mist, visibility was steadily improving.

I wished the same applied to me, but despite there being more important things to think of, like a woman in labour by my side, I'd almost given up caring about anything other than hanging on to the contents of my stomach.

Just as we passed by Alness, Meg put down her knitting, then stretched out her hand and patted mine gently.

'I think, my dear, we should get Charlie to stop.'

20

DELIVERY SERVICE

It was a surreal moment. I was outside the ambulance. The fog had completely cleared and now, under a chandelier of stars with a cold bright moon throwing light down on a bare countryside, I was throwing up.

Unlike here, where the surroundings had all the bleak attraction of a surgical theatre, Charlie and Meg were enjoying a cosy chat in the ambulance. It all sounded rather homely and made me want to get back in again.

Shortly after, and clearing my throat as a sign of restored health, I rejoined the team.

Meg beamed. 'Well, here she comes, and I must say, looking much better too. And, Sister, it's a good thing you popped that plastic sheet under me before you left 'cos I think my waters have broken.' She handed me her knitting, and before I could stop her, she had swung her legs over the side of the couch and stood up. As she stretched she added, 'So, Charlie, maybe it's time to put the foot down.'

'Right!' said Charlie.

'Right,' said I, 'and maybe I should have a wee look, but I can't do that unless you lie down.'

'Right,' said Meg, 'I've never delivered in an ambulance before.'

I could have said that neither had I. It hadn't been on my Belfast midwifery training syllabus where it hadn't been an issue. Readily available transport had always provided quick and easy access to the maternity hospitals.

'Had one last week,' Charlie put in, 'but yon Avoch nurse did cope, and fine.' He chuckled in an admiring way. 'She took it all in her stride and called me a right Charlie for fussing.' As he turned on the engine, he checked his hairstyle was still in place.

'I think he's got a notion for the Avoch girl,' said Meg, putting out a hand to steady me as we rocketed forward. 'He was telling me all about her when you were outside. See if you can put a good word in for him, eh?'

'I'll do what I can, but let's think about *you* for a change, shall we?'

What happened to Dingwall and Muir of Ord, I wondered. I'd been so busy checking on Meg I hadn't noticed Charlie clocking up the miles.

'Ten to go,' he said as we passed through the bonny wee town of Beauly.

Meanwhile, Meg's contractions were getting stronger and she was beginning to squirm.

'Feeling sore?' I asked.

'A bit, but you know, Sister, I've been thinking, I'm sort of worried that if we don't make Raigmore in time and I deliver here they might just tell us to turn around and go home.' For the first time that we'd met, Meg began to look worried.

I recalled my early training days. I'd loved accompanying patients in ambulances transferring them from Aberdeen's Woolmanhill Casualty Department across town to the general hospital. It was really dramatic being in a vehicle that stormed across red traffic lights with lights flashing and siren blaring. Of course, the patient would be ill enough to need more medical attention than the casualty department could offer. However, the journey was long enough to be exciting, yet sufficiently short enough to get the patient in one piece to the right department, and there wasn't time to be travelsick.

This journey was unusual in that my patient who, unless you considered pregnancy an illness, was well but wanted to be admitted into hospital.

I caught a glimpse of a railway line and saw the Beauly Firth on the other side of the road; signs we were getting close to Inverness. Maybe I was going to avoid delivering a baby in a confined space after all. I grew hopeful.

I said, 'If Charlie wasn't belting on I could ask him what happened to the Avoch patient after Ailsa delivered her, but I don't want to take his concentration off the road. Landing in the ditch isn't the best place for a confinement.'

'Oh! That was a bad one!' Meg grabbed my hand. 'Bloody hell!'

Strong language was often a sign that labour was moving into the transitional phase – that point before the mother starts to push.

I'd a quick peek under Meg's blankets, just in case the baby had arrived and hadn't thought to mention it. But it was still a bump, with its mother continuing to grind her teeth. However, we were still on the outskirts of Inverness, with all the signs of an imminent delivery increasing.

'Take deep breaths,' I encouraged. 'Come on, Meg.'

'I'm not going to push,' she groaned.

'Oh, really?'

By this time, I'd resigned myself to this delivery, even got round to marginally looking forward to it. I'd opened the delivery pack, had its contents all ready, and now my patient had opted not to co-operate! She wanted that baby in hospital. I wondered if it was a girl because if she was anything like her mother, it might be a close contest as to who'd decide when and where she'd arrive.

Charlie, picking up on the drama, put his foot down hard. There was no traffic on the road, whilst the town's buildings lay in dark silence as if they too were asleep. It must have given their occupants a rude awakening when the flashing lights and siren were turned on.

A small smile tugged on Meg's lips until another contraction ruled her body.

'Give me strength!' she said, her teeth gritted.

'Nearly there!' cried Charlie, flying the ambulance over the final stretch.

'I'm going to have to push!' Meg groaned, trapping my hand in a vice-like grip.

'Whatever happens, I can't think they'll send you home now,' I squeaked, beginning to worry that my patient was so set on delivering in hospital she wouldn't care where it happened. What if she delivered on a trolley on her way to the Labour Ward?

As we screamed to a halt outside Raigmore's main entrance, two porters, who must have been manning the corridor, ran out pushing a trolley carrying a couple of wooden poles. They glanced up at Charlie, who shouted out of his window. 'Right, boys. Labour Ward. Fast!'

There was a clatter of boots as the men rushed to the ambulance door, threw it open and piled in.

'Here, let me,' I said, helping them to thread the poles into the stretcher cover Meg had been lying on.

A porter puffed out instructions, 'Easy does it. One, two, and . . . three!'

They lifted Meg effortlessly, carried her out of the ambulance and to the accompaniment of her groans, lowered her onto the trolley. Then, they took off, pushing the trolley down the general hospital corridor at such a fast rate I could hardly keep up with them. Carrying Meg's suitcase didn't help, and where was my delivery pack? How could I have forgotten it?

'It's right behind you!' shouted one of the porters. 'Just push!'

'What?' I thought he'd gone mad. Meg's face was bright red, which could only mean one thing. Her groans funnelled down the corridor like something out of a horror movie.

'No! Pant!' I shouted.

The leading porter shoved open the maternity unit doors with his bum. The trolley shot through, with the men now aiming it at the delivery room.

They'd done this before and the same could be said for the couple of midwives taking over. As if Meg's arrival was an everyday occurrence, they lifted her onto a delivery table with practised ease.

'Can Sister here deliver me?' Meg squeezed out the request.

One of the midwives swept a dismissive gaze at my dishevelled form. 'Sister, eh?' She snapped on a pair of rubber gloves as she said, 'Sorry, she's left it a bit late. Now, push!'

'That's four Vass boys now. Quite a handful,' I said to Charlie, driving back to Fearn. 'It's a good thing our patient's got her stay in hospital.'

'I didn't want to say it at the time, but Ailsa's patient wanted to get back home so that's where we took her. I couldn't have said whether or not the hospital would have accepted a delivered baby, but were you worried about delivering her?' Charlie must be tired; he was holding the steering wheel with one finger.

I saw no reason to lie. 'Yes, but not as worried as the way you're driving at the moment.'

'Ah! You girls like a joke. Now that Ailsa one. She can really crack them.' The thought seemed to brighten him, and he put his hands back on the wheel.

'How come you met her? Avoch's surely out of your area.'

'I was helping out,' he explained, 'but I'm thinking of moving nearer Dingwall. It's got a bit more life than Tain, and Strathpeffer's quite near too. Have you ever been to the dances there? They're great.'

'So I've heard. I've believe Fergie Alexander plays there sometimes and he's got a super country dance band.' I thought for a moment, then remembering Meg's request to help Charlie pursue his interest, said, 'Why don't you ask Ailsa to go with you? I bet she loves that kind of dancing.'

'I couldn't do that,' Charlie protested. 'She'd think me awful cheeky.'

'So?' I thought about Ailsa with her dancing curls and mischievous grin then said, 'Look, Charlie, the worst she can do is say no.'

With a grin not dissimilar to Ailsa's, he perked up. 'Aye,' he said, 'Right enough. Maybe I just will. D'you go to dances much yourself?'

'Yeah, sometimes. But right now I'll settle for the bright lights of Fearn. Let's hope we get to see them,' I said, and, hoping Charlie didn't follow by example, I closed my eyes and went to sleep.

21

29 CASTLE TERRACE

In her endless quest to modernise our image, Miss Macleod had got us new coats. They mightn't actually be fashion statements but they were a shade up from navy blue, made in a soft material and had rather classy buttons. The coats' straight-cut design was kind to any figure, but not mine. My coat was hanging on a peg in my Conon Bridge home and I was in Edinburgh.

I must have passed that initial period in Ross-shire well enough to be seconded here to do my official district nurse training. I was now living in the heart of the city along with a group of nine other trainees.

Twenty-nine Castle Terrace was a great address. The building with its high ceilings and elegant proportions must have been intended for grander times. Now it had a more functional role, housing the city's district nurses' headquarters, with lecture rooms and student accommodation on other floor levels above. Nursing equipment and uniforms were stored in the basement, where we were now waiting to be kitted out by Miss Cameron, our tutor.

She pointed to a rack of coats which were like our old Ross-shire gabardine ones, only with a colour so much darker it verged on black. 'We'll do these first. They'll make you conspicuous and immediately recognisable when you're out and about. Of course, and I don't suppose I need to tell you, our profession stands for a caring service. A sensible, tidy appearance plays an important role in all of that.'

Her voice sounded familiar. It must be her Highland accent. As its gentle lilt washed over us, I sensed that shouting wouldn't be her forte. She'd never get a job as a bingo caller. She was far more suited to dealing with people in such a gentle-shepherding sort of way that it made me want to impress her.

Nursing was such a hands-on profession that I hoped that, thanks to Sister Shiach, I'd probably manage the practical aspects of the training all right. Theory might be trickier. I'd just have to wait and see. However, I'd already learnt that the other girls on the course were all very friendly. I felt optimistic.

Spring was in the air despite the searching wind that seemed to be the city's permanent resident. Compared to my old training school's Aberdeen grey and granite, Edinburgh seemed sage and green; the days were stretching and even if our coats looked old fashioned we wouldn't have to wear them when off duty. Then we'd maybe get the time to catch the tail end of the Swinging Sixties. We might be leaving that decade behind but we'd take its music with us. I'd a record of Nina Simone. I loved her voice and had heard she was due to make an appearance soon in the city's Usher Hall.

Then too there were great cinemas. I sighed happily. Here I was in an Edinburgh, firmly on the map thanks to *The Prime of Miss Jean Brodie* film.

I wondered if Miss Cameron, who wore no make-up, had mousy-brown hair styled in finger waves and wore her navy blue box-pleated skirt nearer her ankles than her knees, had seen it. I rather thought she was more likely to enjoy an evening of psalm singing and was determinedly un-swinging.

'Next one please, girls,' she called out.

She was definitely not like Miss Macleod.

The last time I'd seen her, her skirt was even shorter than when I'd had my interview. She'd swapped her specs for contact lenses and her hairstyle verged on the bouffant. There was gossip about a gentleman's clothing frequently appearing on her washing line. Rumours grew but she appeared unaware or indifferent to such talk. I wondered what was going on in her life, but only for a moment. I was too excited thinking about my own in bright city lights.

'You're sure to enjoy yourself in Edinburgh,' Miss Macleod had said, consulting her perfectly manicured fingernails. 'It's a wonderful city. And count yourself lucky. You're going on the last Queen's District Nurse Course. If you pass the exam, you'll be a Queen's Nurse when you come back.'

'*Queen's* Nurse?' I said.

'Yes,' she replied vaguely. 'Started by Queen Victoria, I believe.'

Where was the Sister bit, I wondered. I'd only just got used to the title.

That wasn't an issue with Miss Cameron, but clothing lengths were.

'Good! Not too short,' she said, looking at her class, now rigged out as if ready for a funeral. 'Go ahead and try on a hat. Hopefully the weather'll be fine.' She paused for a moment and I brightened. Maybe if the sun shone we could cast off things which suggested a career in the Desert Foreign Legion, but then Miss Cameron finished. 'And then you won't need to have their lugs down.'

I remembered the Ross-shire pillbox hats with affection. They could be set at a jaunty angle. They could even conceal a few hair rollers fitted under them, handy if, after work, the wearer fancied a night out in Strathpeffer and didn't want to go there with hair hat-flattened. The Edinburgh ones only stayed in one position, were the same colour as our coats and defied any sort of creativity, unless you could do a fancy bow with the ties, there to secure the earflaps to the top of the hat.

'You'll need one of these.' Our tutor pointed to a row of Gladstone bags.

'You must keep them spotlessly clean, and don't forget the cotton linings. They've to be taken out, washed and bleached regularly. You can expect spot-checks on your bags.' She shuddered. 'The last class kept theirs in a disgraceful condition. I even found a packet of fish in one of them. The student said it was for a patient's tea.'

Ignoring our stifled giggles, she warmed to her theme. 'Well, you know, you're all qualified registered nurses so you must know the importance of hygiene and cleanliness, even if some of the homes you visit might challenge those standards.' She squared her shoulders and lifted her chin. Her voice rang out as if marshalling the troops. 'But you must, you must, do your best to keep them. Standards now – they're a must!'

As if surprised by the strength of her eloquence, she paused, giving one girl the chance to look in one of the bags.

'It's easy seen these don't belong to midwives,' she said. 'The toenail scissors, tube and enema funnel are giveaways.'

I wondered if I should mention my recent ambulance trip with Meg Vass but Miss Cameron was ahead of me. 'With a bit of luck,' she said, 'you won't be called to do any midwifery work on this course. I know a few of you have the qualification, but here you'll be covering a district which will have its own midwife. You'll probably not meet her, as she'll be attached to a GP practice. Referrals for their work come from their doctors and maternity units but our work comes from here.' She pointed a finger upwards. I thought she meant Heaven, but she was heading back upstairs. 'Come along,' she called, 'I'll show you. It's part of Headquarters.'

There were grey steel case filing cabinets lining one side of an office where a red telephone made a colourful statement on the secretary's desk. She was just visible behind a huge typewriter with the heavy presence of a steam engine. Momentarily she stopped typing. Without the machine's clatter and ting, the sound of distant buzz of traffic drifted up, reminding us that we were in the centre of a busy city. The building had such a cocoon-like quality it was easy to forget that. Then the telephone rang.

Miss Cameron said, 'As you see, our busy secretary deals with calls as well. They're usually for us from GPs. After she's taken the details and depending on their urgency, she'll either give them to whoever's on call or to the nurse who covers that GP's area.' She pointed to the filing cabinets. 'And these hold the patients' records. As soon as the nurses come back from their visits, they must fill them in.'

I thought about Sister Shiach and her minimalistic record keeping. Here, I suspected, a tick wouldn't suffice.

'Will we be going out on district soon?' someone asked.

'Yes. After a week, and you'll have a district nurse with you as well. She'll check to see you'll manage all right.' Miss Cameron glanced at her watch. 'Good heavens! If we hurry, there's just enough time before lunch to give out your bus passes and let you know the areas you'll be covering. We'll get that done in the classroom.'

Following her stocky frame, we trooped up another flight of stairs and into a big room, light-filled by huge windows looking out on to Edinburgh castle. It was a stunning view but apparently lost on Miss Cameron.

Nodding towards it, she said, 'You know, it's shocking the things that go on over there!' Outrage, magnified by her tortoise-shell-framed spectacles, hardened her eyes into blue stones. She pointed towards the castle's rocky ramparts.

The class as one turned to follow her gaze then burst out

laughing after she conceded, 'Mind you, you'd need binoculars to see them.'

She'd sounded horrified, but now she sucked her bottom lip then, supplicant-like, bent her head. 'Ah well, I'll be talking to you about being non-judgemental and discretion later. Maybe I should start with myself – but,' she added with a righteous sniff, 'modern times aren't always the best.'

She went back to tutor mode, and dusting the sides of her skirt addressed the class as if about to give a huge honour. 'Make it a short lunch break because I'll be showing you how to make Queen's pokes and we'll need plenty time for that. I'm looking forward to getting some really professional work done.'

22

PAPER CHASE

We were waiting for Miss Campbell when she came into the classroom, staggering under the weight of a huge pile of *Sunday Posts*. She thumped them down on a table.

'Oh, I say! Maybe we're going to get a seminar on *The Broons*,' whispered Tina, who was sitting beside me. 'It might help me with the Scottish dialect.'

'I don't think that's a problem for you,' I replied, giving her a friendly nudge. 'After all, even if you are English, you've been a matron in a boys' school there, and I'd think you could cope with anything, never mind our language.'

Tina was unique in our group in that she looked great in the uniform. Her slim figure and blonde, petite good looks must have been a challenge to any hormonally-charged boy under her care.

'What made you want to do district nursing?' I'd asked over the lunch break. 'It must be a world away from school life with all its lovely holidays.'

'Believe you me,' she said, wrinkling her nose, 'they were never long enough. Anyway, I wanted to get back to real life and proper caring.'

'I'm not sure you've come to the right place. I hadn't thought the *Sunday Post* was a font of medical wisdom.'

'Well, that's where you're wrong,' she said. 'What about the letters sent to the *Post*'s doctor's column? I believe they give GPs a clue as to what ailments will be waiting for them on Monday mornings.' She chuckled then put her hands to her lips as Miss Cameron cleared her throat, a discreet sign she was going to begin.

'You're going to find newspapers really useful when you're out on district and, no, they're not for reading on the bus.' She blinked in surprise at the class's ripple of laughter then, looking pleased, continued, 'I'm going to show you how to make a bag from this.' She held up a *Post* and waved it like a banner. 'It'll be something you can put soiled dressings in before you dispose of them. As most of your patients will have coal fires, you'll be able to immediately burn them. It's a proper hygienic method of disposal.'

She beckoned to us with a plump finger. 'It's probably easier if you come up to the table and see how it's done.'

Obediently, we surrounded her. We craned forward with the attention of origami enthusiasts as she spread out two sheets of paper, smoothed, folded, creased and tucked with the expertise and speed of someone with an ironing fetish.

'There! A Queen's poke. See how easy it is!' She held up the finished article.

The *Sunday Post* papers had been transformed into a sturdy bag. It had a certain charm and definite usefulness. It stood on its own, had a wide mouth, a flat base. It even had a lid. Had it not been made of paper it could have made a handy saucepan.

'Now it's your turn,' said Miss Cameron. 'Let's see what you can do.'

As we set to, she adjusted her spectacles and, assuming an air of academic interest, ambled to the window.

'If she's looking for trouble,' muttered Tina, 'she should check up on her class.' But our tutor was lost in her observational station. She seemed deaf to the sound of tearing paper, didn't see screwed up balls of paper aimed into the wastepaper basket or paper darts made efficiently but in a spirit of frustration. But at length, she turned round.

The jumble of shredded paper lying on the table wouldn't have been what she expected.

'Oh dear, it's not usually a problem,' she sighed. Then, reluctantly leaving her post, she came back to the table and took us slowly and with great patience through the process again. And again.

Finally, we managed to get it. Hiding newsprint-blackened fingers behind our backs and standing as proudly as successful bakers, we lined up behind a row of perfectly made Queen's pokes.

'At last!' said our tutor, touching them in a light-fingered gesture of approval. 'Well done. I know you're going to find these handy. Now, has anybody any questions?'

'Em, Miss Cameron,' said Tina, 'why are they called Queen's pokes?'

Miss Cameron looked surprised and a bit discomfited. 'I'm not really sure,' she said. 'Nobody's seen a reason to ask before.'

There was something endearingly innocent about our tutor. I thought that if Miss Macleod had been asked and didn't know, she'd just have spun a yarn.

She seemed a long way away then and two weeks later, so did Dingwall.

For a start, I wouldn't have had to rely on public transport. Here, where people filled the pavements, the morning traffic growled along Princes Street as if complaining at its slow progress. I was waiting for a bus, and with none in sight, began to worry that I was going to be late for my first patient on my own – not an auspicious start.

I wondered how the rest of the class was managing. After our first week with Miss Cameron, we'd spent the next one shadowing a district nurse. We must have done all right because we were now, complete with bus passes, street maps and a list of patients' names and addresses, all out on our own rounds.

'Check the nursing notes beforehand. Then you'll get an idea of what to expect and what needs to be done,' said Miss Cameron, looking at us over the top of her spectacles. 'And, Nurse Macpherson, your first patient is Mrs Henderson. There's quite a lot to read about her in the notes because she's been on our list for so long. You'll not manage to read everything about her, so just give the recent notes a scan to grasp the essentials. You can catch up with her full history afterwards.'

It had taken me longer to decipher the handwritten notes than I'd planned. Now, still with no bus in sight, I tried not to panic that I might have wasted time. I gazed skyward. High above and dominating the skyscape, the castle glowered down, making my thoughts drift back to the weekend.

David, my old school pal, had come through from his work in Glasgow and we'd gone to see round the ancient fortress. There Edinburgh's history reached up and enfolded us, whilst we fell into the familiar ways of a friendship moving towards something far more interesting.

The signs were there as, hand in hand, we strolled towards the Castle Gardens. Their winding paths took us through a park where rabbits scampered through trees and weed-filled long grass. Lacking the manicured perfection of the Princes Street Gardens, the park had instead a rustic charm. But no seats.

'This'll have to do.' David took off his jacket, and after spreading it on the ground, sat down. Patting a space left on it, he said, 'Lovely view from here.'

'Some view! ' I said, joining him and squinting up at the sky. 'One minute I'm looking down on the Scott Monument and the next I can only see clouds. Ow!' I shot back into the standing position. 'I've been stung.'

Too late I saw a nettle patch, small enough to be inconspicuous but big enough to cause my sudden levitation. I rubbed my leg, beginning to regret that I was wearing that killer mini-skirt I'd broken the bank to buy. 'You must have seen them,' I yelped.

'Well, as a matter of fact I didn't but, och, you'll be fine,' he said, then laughed and lay back, cushioning his head with his hands. The sun beat down, a cloud drifted past and he closed his eyes. 'Go and see if you can find a docken. They're supposed to be good for stings.'

'It's just as well you're not the nurse,' I said and made to go and look for one, when he caught my ankle.

'Gotcha!'

I crashed down. It was a soft landing but not from David's point of view.

'You nearly flattened me,' he gasped. 'Get off!'

'That's not very chivalrous.' I got up once more. 'So where's a nice knight in shining armour when you need one, pray?'

'Here!' he wheezed.

At last, strategically avoiding the nettles, I made a final descent.

With his eyes full of mischief and his arms stretched out, David cried out in best Glasgow, 'And she's going down for the third time!'

A startled blackbird that'd been eyeing us with keen interest flew from a nearby tree, leaving us in a pleasant silence. Momentarily I wondered if Miss Cameron was scanning the horizon, then forgot.

A little later we grew cold. Clouds began to gather in a way that threatened rain. Shivering, David got up and put his jacket back on. 'I know,' he said as if suddenly struck by a monumentally clever plan, 'why don't we go back to your place? I fancy a wee lie down. I'd a really early start to get here.'

I stared at him. 'You mean, back at the home?'

'Yeah. Why not?'

I brushed grass off my skirt to give myself a bit of time to think, whilst imagining the conversation. 'Ooh, hello, Miss Cameron,' I'd say, dead casual. 'Look! I found this nice young man in my bedroom. Seems a decent sort of chap. He wants to stay the night. I know it's only a single bed, but I'm happy to share.' Then I'd nudge her in the ribs and say in a jokey way she was bound to find irresistible, 'We Highlanders know a thing or two about hospitality, don't we?'

The picture faded as reality kicked in and I snapped, 'You must be joking. No bloke would be allowed past the front door.'

'You could easily smuggle me in. For goodness' sake, where's your spirit of adventure, Janie?' He laughed in the infectious way I usually found endearing, but not this time.

'I'd get fired if you were caught,' I retorted, 'if our tutor didn't die of heart failure first.'

He shrugged, then said, 'Oh well, I know you and if you've made up your mind, there's nothing I can say to get you to change it.' He jingled change in his pocket and looked worried. 'And as that's the case, I'd best get back to Glasgow. I can't afford to stay the night.' Glancing at his watch, he grumped, 'So if I go now, I suppose I'll get a bus.'

I didn't stop him. Now, standing waiting for my own bus to come along, I wished that I had, or at least that we'd parted on better terms.

23

HILDA SHOWS HOW

I got back to the more immediate present. I was beginning to think I'd never get to Mrs Henderson. I understood from the nursing notes that she'd had a stroke several years ago which had left her bed-bound with a left-sided paralysis. Her epileptic daughter who'd cared for her had suddenly died. Since then, the district nursing service had given general nursing care, with the recent notes describing a simple service of helping her to keep clean, comfortable and well enough to stay at home.

I didn't recall mention of a home help and wondered if she had one. At this rate, she might be thinking she hadn't a nurse either. I fretted, hardly believing it when a bus did eventually pull up.

As I boarded it I gave the street name to the conductor and asked him to let me know when we were there. He laughed and said, 'I'll give you a shout, pal, but if you don't mind me saying so, district nurses usually know where they're going.' Grinning, he returned my bus pass.

What a fine thing this is, I thought, putting it back in my pocket. It was like having freedom of the city. Maybe there was something to be said about public transport after all. I was glad I hadn't taken my car. Even in the Sixties, Edinburgh's parking was a problem.

*   *   *

My district, with its poorly-curtained, grime-stained tenements, was a long way from Princes Street and a gentrification which would transform it in the future. A horse-drawn milk float would be a rare sight nowadays, but nobody thought much about it then. The fine white one standing outside Mrs Henderson's address was a regular, with a milkman already lifting out two bottles of milk from their crate. He handed them to me. 'Would you take that in to Mrs Henderson? She's in the basement. You'll save me the steps and my legs.'

With a twinkle, he nodded at mine then spoke to the horse, 'Very nice but you'll notice she's no sugar for you – not even polio ones.' He stroked the horse's nose. 'And they call it a caring profession!'

He made me laugh as I went down the dark stone stairs, footsteps clattering. A dank smell lingered, whilst something soft brushed over my foot. It might have been a rat, and the woman with her rodent-like features who answered the door could have been a relation.

'It's just the nurse,' she called over her shoulder. Then, addressing me directly, she said, 'Come on in. I'm Hilda, the home help.' Patting her headsquare bristling with rollers underneath, she led me into an ill-lit room dominated by a large bed and radiogram.

A small fire sulked in a tiled fireplace. Hilda, moving on thin, scampering legs, went to the highly polished coalscuttle. Ignoring its shovel, she lifted out a lump of coal and threw it on the fire. That would explain her grimed hands, but I wasn't sure about the mark on her arm. It was more like a bruise and I only saw it because she'd pulled up her sleeve. She hauled it back down, looking cross, aware of my glance.

'So you're our new student.' A voice came from the bed I'd thought unoccupied. A thin veined hand came out from under colourless felted blankets and fingers twiddled in welcome.

'Hilda'll get you the basin.' The woman in the bed seemed lost and helpless in the vastness of that bed but her voice was strong, with a warmth as if a chuckle ran through it.

'Whoops!'

Hilda had bent over the tiny form and with practised ease, punching feather pillows into supportive submission, brought Mrs Henderson up to eye level. She had a pale face, pointed chin, scanty grey locks, bright enquiring eyes and looked like a friendly wizard – but maybe not a very good one. The muscle contractures pulling her leg and arm into the frozen foetal position of her left side made it look as if she'd been in the middle of a spell that had gone wrong.

'There! Won't be a minute.' Hilda sped off, her high heels clicking on the brown linoleum floor.

She was fast. I'd no sooner swapped my coat for the uniform-protecting plastic apron hanging shroud-like at the back of the bedroom door than she'd returned. With the important bearing of someone carrying state jewels, she carried a threadbare towel, face flannel and an enamel basin with green soap floating in it.

'Whatever you do, remember you're a guest in every patient's house and that's a privilege. I know it can be difficult but accept whatever's available and don't ask too many questions.' I knew from my experience with Jock and Willie that these words didn't always apply, but now as both Sister Shiach and Miss Cameron's words came back, I obeyed them to the letter. Under Hilda's watchful eye, I carefully set about my task.

'You're doing fine,' she said as I coaxed a lather from the soap and tried to ease the flannel under the armpit of my patient's paralysed arm.

'The nurses always have a job with this,' Mrs Henderson said, nodding at her arm as if it didn't belong to her. 'Of course, some are better than others.' Judgement lay there, so it might not be the time to say the soap was the kind my granny used to wash her woollens and greasy marks off the floor. Anyway, my patient's skin looked wonderful, and I said so.

Mrs Henderson beamed, laughter lines lighting her face. 'Aye, if I was in hospital the starchy sheets would have finished me. I'd have had bedsores by the dozen.' She stretched out her working hand and saluted Hilda. 'She's my saviour.'

'Ach! Away with you. You're always saying that,' said Hilda. 'You know fine it's my job.' She searched in her crossover pinny for a hanky, trumpeting into it so loudly the sound bounced off the distempered walls.

'D'you ever get out of bed, Mrs Henderson?' I asked.

The question wouldn't be asked today, since few patients are left bed-bound, helping to avoid the contractures which so limited my patient. But in those long-ago training days, it was considered okay for patients to stay in bed. With only the occasional outing to the commode beside it, I thought Mrs Henderson must find it a long day.

'No, no!' She chuckled. 'There's Hilda, and my son comes home at dinner time, then the twins are here after school.'

'Twins?'

Identical girls with neatly plaited hair and wearing immaculate school uniforms beamed out from a framed photograph sitting on the ancient music machine. As a piece of furniture it had all the attractive qualities of a coffin.

'Orphans,' Mrs Henderson was off-hand. 'Now that my daughter's away, Hilda, my son and I bring them up.' A grin flashed across her thin face. 'And one thing they can depend on is that their Gran's always at home for them.'

'Yes. Keep them in order, you do,' Hilda put in. 'They don't get out of the house until you've had a good look to see if they're tidy and done their homework.'

I was full of admiration. 'Seems to me you hardly need a nurse.'

'Well you girls need to get your training,' said my patient, 'and I always look forward to your Miss Cameron's visit. She'll be coming with you for your final exam. We always have a great catch-up.' She drew a deep breath and twiddled with the sheet hem-end. 'I'm always teasing her about getting a man.'

Hilda took a duster from her overall pocket and flicked it in the direction of the radiogram.

'I think she's a bit of a nosey parker,' she said with a sniff. 'Why doesn't she mind her own business and stay back at base? I'm sure we could test you girls ourselves.'

I wondered about Hilda's bruise. It was neither the time nor place to inquire about it.

As I headed for my next patient, the words came floating back. 'Don't ask too many questions.' I'd have to wait until I got back to Castle Terrace.

24

IT TAKES ALL SORTS

I wasn't due back at Castle Terrace until lunchtime, and despite the late start, I had got through the morning's work with some spare time left. Grabbing a moment of freedom, I caught the first bus coming my way. The conductor didn't ask where I was going, which was just as well. If I'd said I was having a little jaunt, he might have put in a complaint about bus pass abuse to Miss Cameron.

The top of the double decker gave a great view as we rattled over cobbled streets where wall plaques on buildings with crow-step gables testified to Edinburgh's colourful historical past. The Brutalist features of the present Sixties buildings made more futuristic statements. Passing those concrete cold angular blocks, I wondered would they someday merit plaques and would time ever mellow such harsh lines.

I thought about one of my patients, who lived in a flat on the top floor of a high rise. He seemed lonely and isolated but perhaps he kept himself away from people because he'd TB and had grown used to the initial-prescribed quarantine time. He was thin to the point of emaciation. A needle going into so little flesh must be painful.

'Streptomycin's not the best injection in the world,' I'd said. 'I'm sorry this injection's too big to go into your arm and has to go into your hip.'

I supposed that being subjected to that, as well as having to lower your trousers in front of someone much, much younger, could be unnerving, but he had a stoical calm and a gentle dignity.

'I know, and it's no bother. It's how the other nurses have done it. They jabs are to be given long-term and I've got used to them,' he said. Looking out of the un-curtained window, he pulled his trousers back up again. 'You did fine.'

He didn't invite conversation so I left him, feeling that I'd abandoned him in a barren little room under a cloud of personal sadness and that I'd been unable to think of a way to change it. Edinburgh life was exciting, but remembering Miss Caird, my Raigmore lady, I realised people could as easily isolate themselves in a city as in a Highland glen.

I was so wrapped in thought I hadn't noticed there were no other passengers left in the bus and when it stopped, the driver switched off the engine. I hurried downstairs as the conductor took off his cap and threw it onto a seat.

'We're not going any further,' he announced.

'Gosh! That was quick,' I said, not bargaining on arriving at the bus depot. 'I hadn't noticed where we were. I should've got out at the last stop.'

I leapt down the bus steps, and assuming the walk of a very busy important person, hurried away. With a bit of luck, and out of depot sight, I'd get the next bus back into town.

I'd to wait longer than I'd hoped. Now, breathlessly, I tumbled into the office. The other girls were already there and, watched over by Miss Cameron, writing up their case notes. She glanced up. 'Ah!' she said, 'we were beginning to think you were lost. No problems, I hope?'

I searched for my pen and pulled out Mrs Henderson's notes from the filing cabinet. 'Some poor connections, I'm afraid, but I think I'm getting the hang of things.'

'How did you get on there?' Miss Cameron stood at my shoulder.

I told her what I thought was relevant, then, suspecting the next bit mightn't be so welcome, lowered my voice. 'I noticed Hilda had a bruise on her arm and am sure she didn't want me to see it.'

The tutor's shoulders drooped and she sighed. 'She and Mrs Henderson make a great team and it works both ways.' She dropped her voice into a whisper, 'But as for bruises, Hilda hates when I ask her how she is. Reckons I'm prying. But you know, I think that strangely enough, the Hendersons' house is something of a refuge for her. Weekends especially.'

Despite the pain flickering across her homely face, I could tell by her tone of voice that the subject was closed. Scotland would have to wait some more years before domestic abuse was sufficiently recognised to establish Womens' Refuges, but in 1969 Mrs Henderson was doing her supportive bit.

Meanwhile, Miss Cameron was moving on. 'So what about Miss Crawford? You know she's an old matron?' She widened her eyes and looked innocent.

Did I know! Not half! But much as I wanted to, I didn't say, 'I reckon that old biddy's a chancer.' I thought about an old, fat, cross-faced woman sprawled in a high bed in a stiflingly hot room, alone but for the company of a pug dog whom I'd had to wash around. Unlike Miss Forbes, who desperately wanted to be up and coping independently in Muir of Ord, Miss Crawford had retired to her bed and by all accounts was refusing to leave it.

When I'd visited her, she'd immediately set the tone. 'Nurses nowadays have no idea of how to set about proper bed bathing. You're new, but I don't suppose you'll be any different.'

When I brought a basin of water and put it on her bedside table, she stuck an index finger into it. 'Told you! You plainly haven't used a thermometer. That's so hot you'll scald me. What'd you say, Bobo?' She caressed the head of the dog curled up beside her.

At least there was one bed occupant who seemed friendly. He got up, moved his body as if in welcome, then, snuffling cosily, settled back down again whilst I went off to look for face flannels. I could only find one.

When I got back to my patient I held it up, saying, 'The water should be fine now, and is this your face cloth?' I was surprised that someone from the Old School hadn't half a dozen and that this one should smell so vile.

'Of course,' she said, screwing up her eyes to squint at it. 'What else would it be, you stupid girl?'

In full non-judgemental mode, I carried on, concentrating on a fair acreage of flesh but missing out her face since the pug was happily doing it instead.

'Thanks, Bobo,' she said, looking better pleased than when I suggested it was time to wash her bottom.

The word triggered off a reaction so aggressive that Bobo, coming out in sympathy, growled.

'How dare you use that word!' she shrilled. 'The correct term is *lower back*. You should know that. What kind of training school did you go to?' She put her hands over her head and groaned in despair, 'I wouldn't have to be telling you this if you'd trained in the hospital where I was matron.'

I'd only met Mrs Henderson for the first time today, but I reckoned she'd never speak to anybody like this. Whilst Miss Crawford might live in comfortable wealth in a better part of my district, I thought that in terms of sociability, she was poverty stricken.

After the bathing was accomplished as best I could, she sighed, and wiping her brow as if she'd come through a major trauma, she stroked Bobo for comfort. 'Well! I'm glad that's over. What d'you say, Bobo?'

I almost expected the dog to reply but he was taking a lot more interest in the face cloth. Very politely but firmly, he took it and held it as if it was his own.

With a look of dawning horror, Miss Crawford grabbed it, then with the force of an accomplished cricket bowler, lobbed it over the side of the bed, screaming, 'Nurse! You've been using Bobo's cloth!'

Recalling the incident, I wondered what Miss Cameron would say if I gave her the true facts, but was saved from saying anything because she went into musing mood. 'Miss Crawford's bound to know that lying in bed all the time's bad for her. We only went in after she'd a bad dose of flu to help get her over it. Of course, now she's become over-dependent on us and being a matron from the Old School,' she smiled apologetically, 'she's used to getting her way. I don't know how we can get her to change.'

I could have told her that I could. Not only had it been successful in getting our patient to leap out of bed, but it had given her an impetus to leg it to the bathroom. Miss Cameron might be as surprised as I was to learn that Miss Crawford could easily manage to use her shower and to do it herself. Instead, I went for a light-hearted diplomacy. 'It can't be easy being on your own most of the time. Maybe being an old matron can damage your health.'

The tutor giggled then blushed as if levity was a sin. 'Yes,' she said, 'I don't think I'd like to be one. I rather lead than command. Now go and catch up on your notes.'

Wondering what I should write about Miss Crawford, I settled for something as bland as had previously been written. Clearly nobody wanted to mess with an ex-matron and I hadn't wanted to hang about after she was safely out of the shower. I wondered would there be a fallout and suspected trouble could be heading my way.

Reading the fascinating notes on Mrs Henderson shifted my thoughts. I learnt that the twins and their birth had been as big a surprise to everyone as was, seven years later, their mother's death. Immobilised in her bed, Mrs Henderson had seen both.

Clinically, the notes recorded nursing intervention, dealing with her shock and subsequent declining health. Then, there was a small footnote mentioning Hilda. Coupled with her appearance and perhaps the twins' growth and dependence, Mrs Henderson had improved. No mention was made of the twins' father, which remained a mystery. It's only now I wonder who he was. Nor was I curious about Mrs Henderson's son. The notes didn't mention him other than he was a relation. I only knew that he worked and when he came home to the flat, she said he helped.

Happily for my young and big ego, Mrs Henderson seemed far more interested in me. In the following days, I brought her my news from an outside world denied to her.

'I'm going to a Nina Simone concert tonight,' I told her one day. 'She's going to be in the Usher Hall.' I gently dabbed my patient's face dry with a towel, wishing it wasn't as hard as the colour of its stripes, then went on, 'I can't wait to hear her. She's a wonderful singer. Plays the piano too.'

'I expect it's modern stuff. More the twins' style,' scoffed Hilda. But Mrs Henderson looked thoughtful. She moved restlessly. 'D'you think they'd like her?'

I was dubious about the radiogram but it was one way to find out if it was ever used. 'I've got an LP of hers and if you like, I could bring it. Then you could hear her too. See what she sounds like.'

A flush of pleasure warmed her face. 'Now *I'll* have some news to tell the girls for a change.'

25

LONG LIVE THE QUEEN'S POKES!

The Usher Hall is on Edinburgh's busy Lothian Road. Traffic adds congestion but any passer-by who hasn't stopped to admire the concert hall's imposing frontage should. I had, and wondered what it looked like inside. Tonight would bring the answer.

I got ready early, but knowing I'd a ticket, I dawdled the short distance from Castle Terrace only to see a worryingly long queue snaking down the road. I checked my watch as I joined the line. Half an hour before blast off!

'Fully booked!' The words travelled down the line, person to person. Those who hadn't tickets stayed put, whilst the rest of us, trying not to look smug, passed them. Still, they seemed happy enough to be waiting in a biting wind on the chance of getting a late entry.

They must have been disappointed. The concert hall was packed. There was such a babble from the audience's excited voices travelling round the curved walls it was hard to imagine the place ever being silent, but soon after I sat down, the noise was cut as if thrown by a switch.

Unannounced, an elegant figure glided on stage. Nina Simone appeared luminescent in a long shimmering dress with the lights catching the pearls in her piled-up hair and glinting on her long dangling earrings. She bowed to the burst of applause, moved to the grand piano and touched it as if greeting an old friend.

When she sat down and began to play, the audience stilled. The notes floated out, wrapping us into one listening body. Then she began to sing.

I had never heard anything so lovely. Her smoky voice curled around each listener as if giving a personal message. The line of her song began, 'My baby don't care for shows.' The effect was electrifying.

The audience sat, bewitched by the figure bent over the keyboard. We might not have known what it meant but all recognised the mystery of soul music.

It was an extraordinary performance and brought a normally restrained people to its feet. But however crowded and grand the Usher Hall with its ornate cornices and plush seats was, it could not have held a more appreciative audience than the humble room I was in the following day.

'I've polished the record player,' said Hilda, taking the record from me and removing its cover. I was too late to suggest she keep her fingers clear of the vinyl for she'd already lifted the record player's lid, blown dust off the turntable and lowered the record into place. 'There!'

Despite the record player's aged needle having to plough through Hilda's fingerprints and hissing on play throughout, it was no distraction to a spellbound Mrs Henderson. Her right-hand fingers tapped out the rhythm as if she too were a pianist. Even the fire flames seemed to cheer up and dance higher, whilst Hilda had the far-off look of someone visiting an enchanted place.

'I've got life,' Nina's mellow voice eventually ended on that song.

Silence fell, then was broken by the sound of the needle veering out of the record's grooves. Whilst Hilda rushed to lift it off, Mrs Henderson patted my hand with her good one.

'And I've still got my boobies too,' she grinned, taking a line from the song. 'I think the girls will like it too. Will you leave us with the record for a few days, Nurse Jane?'

Miss Macleod would have had a fit at the informality, and so, I imagined, would Miss Cameron. She'd certainly not have expected general nursing care to be accompanied by the songs of a jazzy-blues singer, but a routine had been established. Mrs Henderson was keen to get more Simone records, Hilda happy to help and the twins were making a bid for The Rolling Stones. General nursing care in the Henderson house was never going to be the same again.

Perhaps if I got a new patient I'd manage to be more professionally correct. I might even get a chance to use a Queen's poke.

I got the chance the following week when Miss Cameron bent a blue gaze on me.

'Apparently Miss Crawford's decided to get out of bed. She says she's fully recovered. Doesn't need our service. Now, isn't that strange?'

On my rounds I'd glimpsed Miss Crawford walking Bobo, who was giving a lamp post the same level of interest he'd given his facecloth. The best I could manage was, 'Um.'

It had been miraculous seeing the old lady out during the day. I suspected that to keep the real state of her health a secret, she'd have previously taken the dog out at night, but it was also worrying that she might have told Miss Cameron about the face cloth. I held my breath. The tutor clasped her hands together as if about to give a sermon.

Here goes, I thought, relieved if startled when she said, 'You know Miss Macleod has mentioned you'd quite a reputation for helping your patients towards independence. "Unusual methods," she said.' For a moment, the tutor looked thoughtful then continued, 'So in place of Miss Crawford, I'd like you to visit Mrs

Collins. See how you get on dressing her leg ulcer. Apparently she's been treating it herself for the past few months but has at last admitted to her doctor it's not getting any better.'

I should have realised Miss Macleod would be making contact with Castle Terrace. After all, time was passing and she'd want her staff member back, qualified. Soon we'd be taking our final exam where the emphasis would be on the practical side. Knowing that Miss Cameron would be the examiner, I hoped to finally achieve a truly professional approach with one patient at least. Mrs Collins, her leg and some finely honed Queen's pokes might give me that chance.

I was full of good intentions on making that first visit. My patient lived in a tenement flat. Going through its main entrance, I thought how few visits I paid to patients who lived in houses. If I hadn't had an aunt living in genteel poverty in a Morningside one, I might have thought Edinburgh houses were reserved for only the very rich and healthy.

Meanwhile, I climbed up stone steps so clean they looked like they'd been recently scrubbed. And they were worn, as if by thousands of feet. But the silence in the building said it was giving nothing away whilst no sound escaped through the heavy doors of the flats I plodded past.

The Collins name stood out on a plaque under a brass doorknocker. Both shone in burnished splendour out of a newly painted black door. The noise of its rapper seemed like a gross intrusion in that silent stairwell space, but as soon as the door was opened, a shout of welcome rang out.

'You'll be the nurse. I'm not really needing one, but come in anyway.'

Even if she hadn't said that, I'd still have known she was my patient. The bandaged leg was the giveaway. Otherwise she could,

161

with her round figure, white hair and pink cheeks, have been mistaken for Granny Bun of *Happy Families*.

Despite her only accepting our service with reluctance, her welcome seemed genuine. She beckoned me into a room where the black lead fire-range had had much the same loving attention lavished on it as the brass fittings on the door. The sun streamed in through the top part of a sash window, its light diffusing through impressively white lace netting strung on a rod across the bottom half.

'Sit down, sit down!' She switched off the television and pointed to a chair matching the mock leather sofa where a small boy sat.

'Aw, Granny!' he said, shaking his carrot-coloured hair in annoyance. 'I was watching that.'

Resigned to boredom, he began to twiddle his Clarks shoes, exploring his nose with a careful finger and sliding back and fore over the sofa's highly polished surface.

'Well, you're not now. Go and play upstairs.'

The response was quick. 'You haven't got an upstairs and it was *The Clangers!*'

''I'll clang you, Tom,' said his grandmother, aiming a casual blow in his general direction. 'Just you wait till your mum gets in from work. Honestly, the sooner you go to school, the better it'll be for my health. Anyway, nurse here isn't going to be long, are you?' Her voice, if kindly, was anxious.

Tom stuck out his bottom lip and folded his arms, his eyes just visible and glaring out from under his long fringe, resentment filling the air. I was an intrusion. Mrs Collins looked anxious. Despite her tuts at Tom, I knew that if it came to a toss between loyalties, I'd be the loser. If I wanted to get back here, I'd need to think of something quick.

I went to sit beside Tom. 'You don't have any comics by any chance?'

162

He stopped sliding for a moment whilst his granny looked surprised. 'Well, there's last week's *Dandy*. Look, it's right by you.'

'Great,' I spread the paper on my knee. 'Can I show you something, Tom?'

He looked at it in contempt and folded his arms. He really did a lovely pout. 'Granny's read it to me already.'

'Ah! But it's perfect for this,' I said, and with many a theatrical flourish, conjured up a Queen's poke.

Tom wasn't going to be impressed. 'So?' His look was challenging. 'What's it for?'

I could hardly say it was for burning so I held it up as if it was an objet d'art.

'It's a boat, silly! Anybody can see that. Now you could make one, take it to the bathroom and see if you can sail it in the sink, and if not, you could try bombarding it with soap. See how long it takes you to sink it. But, Tom,' I knew by his bright green eyes fixed on the poke that he was interested. 'I bet you can't make one.'

He was scornful and jumped off the sofa. 'Huh! That's easy.'

With Tom more gainfully engaged at a table, Mrs Collins lay on the sofa whilst I undid her bandage.

'I bet you don't often sit, never mind stretch out,' I said. 'You keep this place so spotless. I've never seen anywhere cleaner.'

Looking at the raw inflamed sore, I could have said, 'Or a worse-looking ulcer,' but perhaps the Sofra-Tulle dressing Mrs Collin's doctor had prescribed would help. I laid the antibiotic-impregnated gauze dressing, explaining its magical properties, and finished the dressing.

'I know it can't be easy, but when you do sit down, it's really good if you can keep your leg up,' I said, popping the soiled dressing into the poke and slinging it into the fire.

Tom looked up from the table, his jaw dropped. 'What did you do that for? I thought we were going to have a competition. See who'd be the first to sink their boat.' Resting his elbows on the table, he put his hands over his head. 'Anyway, I can't make mine,' he said, trying to rub away a tell-tale tear. 'It's rubbish.'

26

TIME FOR SOME
PATIENTS' SUPPORT

Mrs Collins had been lying on the sofa looking at her feet as if she hadn't seen them from this angle lately. Hearing Tom, she struggled to her feet. 'Shh! Don't be such a softie. Look, I'm sure I could have a go. Nurse's far too busy to show you again.'

At the sight of a small boy in distress, formality went out of the window. 'I'm not so busy that I can't show you again, Tom,' I said, joining him at the table. 'Anyway, Mrs Collins, you'll need to learn how to make them the proper way as well. So please sit down again and watch. *And keep that leg up.*' I turned to Tom. 'Now, whenever you see your gran sitting down, you just remind her to do that in case she forgets.'

'Sure will.' Tom brightened. 'But I'm only here in the mornings. Who'll mind her after that?'

Mrs Collins laughed. 'I'll be fine. I've nobody here to look after but myself.' She nodded at a photograph of a man in a flat cap looking sternly out from a highly polished silver frame. 'Now that my Norman's gone.' She sighed and looked out of the window for a moment. 'I do miss him. He was right good at scrubbing the stairs.'

'I take it you do them now?' I was casual.

'Of course. I take my turn.' She sounded defensive.

'I'll be back at the end of the week,' I said, leaving the flat a little later than planned. As I went down the steps I was sure that Mrs Collins cleaned them more often than she admitted, but I couldn't think of a way to change that. Remembering Tom's armada of Queen's pokes was much more satisfying.

Hands on hips, he'd surveyed them with a big grin whilst his granny said, 'Now that's what I call ship-shape. Maybe you'll be a sea captain when you grow up.'

Tom narrowed his eyes and stuck out his chest as he strutted back to the sofa. Tucking in beside Mrs Collins, he said, 'And I bet you I'll be good at sinking them too. I'll show you how tomorrow but, Granny, let's just sit and watch telly *so you can rest that leg.*'

Throughout the course, clinical instructors had occasionally accompanied us on our rounds. They were experienced district nurses, qualified in teaching best practice, and were so friendly and helpful it was easy to forget that we were students. However, our practical exam, watched over by Miss Cameron, was bound to be different.

'Would you mind a visit from Miss Cameron?' I asked Mrs Henderson. 'Our practical exam's next week and she says she'd like to catch up with you as well as see how I manage caring for you.'

'As if I didn't,' said Hilda, banging down a basin so that the water slopped over the edge. 'Honestly! I should sit that exam. I bet I'd pass with flying colours.' She rolled her eyes and stomped out of the bedroom, her high heels sounding like castanets racky-tacking.

'Don't worry about Hilda,' said Mrs Henderson. 'She's just getting over a bad weekend. I know you're going to be fine. We haven't had a failure yet.'

Mrs Collins was just as reassuring. She looked pleased when

I'd said Miss Cameron had especially asked to see her. 'Apparently your leg might be the highlight of her day,' I told her. 'She wants to see how well I dress it.'

'Och! You'll pass with flying colours, and Nurse,' she said, taking my arm and looking at me earnestly, 'don't you worry about Tom. You'll never believe it but the couple in that flat opposite noticed you were calling. They came and offered to take him to Blackford Pond so that he could get a proper sail for his paper boats. Actually, I think he prefers terrorising the swans,' she gave an unconvincing tut, then went on, 'but he comes back happy as Larry, with colour in his cheeks too, and as well as that, my neighbours say he's great company and saves the pair of them from sitting at home getting bored with each other.'

'Did you know them before?'

'No. Not really. Norm and me always kept ourselves to ourselves.' Mrs Collins spoke slowly. 'Maybe we should have been a bit more like them. They're using their retirement to help other folk. D'you know, they're even taking my turn on the stairs till my leg gets better.'

'Well, it's certainly on the mend. All that rest you're giving it's doing it good. Look, Mrs Collins, before you know where you are, you'll be off walking to Blackford Park with your new pals. You'll just not need to sprint for the first wee while.'

Mrs Collins had a pewter tray. I was worried that the paper bag holding all the dressings hadn't looked professional but hadn't wanted to imply criticism. Now that we'd a comfortable relationship, I asked if we could use the tray.

'It would be more hygienic and we'd see what was there,' I'd explained. 'Then I can see what's needed before we run out.'

'Certainly. What a good idea. I'll give it a good clean and it'll be ready for you tomorrow. We're a team, you and me,' she'd said.

I was touched by the way she'd thrown herself into the spirit of things. She'd provided a spotless damask hand towel to cover the tray's dimpled base, her finest Tupperware containers for the gauze swabs, cotton wool and crepe bandages. The bottle of Savlon and a random appearance of zinc and castor oil jar might have thwarted her a bit, but she rallied with the Sofra-Tulle and plastic apron. 'I've put them on bonny plates,' she said, 'and I'll always be sure to have a pan boiling to sterilise your forceps.'

I looked at the tray. 'My tutor will think she's getting a cup of tea,' I said.

Tea was probably the last thing on Miss Cameron's mind as I introduced her to Mrs Collins, who said, 'I'm sorry there's only one good chair.' With the cheerfulness of the floating-through-the-air-with-a-wand Cookeen Fairy advertisement, she showed her to the mock-leather chair. It had been so well polished that Miss Cameron sat down, then, fearing she might fall off, took a tight grip of its arms.

Oblivious to anything but being the perfect patient, Mrs Collins, wreathed in smiles, lay on the sofa. 'I always lie here. Nurse Macpherson says I've got to rest with my legs up.' I thought the imitation mischievous, but Mrs Collins was unstoppable. 'She's a caution, says I need to improve my reading.' She picked up and waved a copy of *The Scotsman*. 'And this makes better boats as well.'

'Ha ha, I think you mean *poke*,' I said, advancing with the tray and setting to my task.

Blithely, my patient continued, 'I wasn't for having a nurse, but I can see how daft that was. My leg's fair come on since she started dressing it. Look.'

Gingerly, Miss Cameron eased herself forward. 'Yes, that looks fine, healing round the edges – always a good sign.' She sat back quickly, then ventured, 'Tell me, Mrs Collins, do you ever wear support stockings?'

Blast! I'd never thought of that.

Miss Cameron continued, 'They're a good idea. They really help with circulation. I wear Elbeos.' Knuckles white on the chair arms, she risked stretching out her legs and looking at them complacently. 'I have done since I started nursing training. With all our work keeping us on our feet, I thought I'd be prone to problems like varicose veins, so often the curse of our profession.' Tucking those well cared for pins under the chair, she added, 'Look after your legs, I say.'

Hoping mine without the Elbeo bonus weren't about to fall off, I finished the dressing with much smiling and sly winking from Mrs Collins. I hadn't bargained on a discussion involving Miss Cameron's legs, but there certainly was nothing wrong with their agility.

Visit over, the tutor practically shot off the chair. 'Thank you so much for your co-operation,' she said, heading for the door. 'And remember, those stockings really do help.'

I was hard pushed to keep up with her as she skipped back down the tenement stairs.

At their foot, she glanced at her watch. 'We'll easy walk the distance. It's probably quicker than taking a bus.' She sniffed the air and took a deep breath. 'I must say it's good to get away from being stuck inside, and I always enjoy meeting the patients. But we mustn't linger. Let's go.' She set off, her arms and box-pleated skirt swinging as if she was a marching Wren.

I'd grown to love my district with all its variety of patients. Their wry humour and stoic outlook played a big part in helping them cope with their different ailments. But even if the area was rich in character, it couldn't always hide its poverty.

Passing a pawn shop, Miss Cameron noted, 'I bet there's not too many of them up north.'

I could have said the same might apply to the shabby-looking place we were approaching and reputed to be a knocking shop, but as she sped past she took my mind completely off it.

'How will you get on in Fortrose?' she asked.

'Fortrose?'

She stopped for a moment, turned round and blinked at me in her earnest way. 'Yes, Miss Macleod was telling me there's soon going to be a vacancy there. Of course, you'll know it's on the Black Isle. Handy for Inverness and, personally, I think it would suit you very nicely.'

I was so surprised I must have just gaped. I knew there was a vacancy coming up there but hadn't dared to think I'd get it. Mulling it over, I'd to practically run after Miss Cameron who, as if regretting discussing my future, had hurried off again.

But at least she took the time to wait outside Mrs Henderson's house. Usually I clattered down the steps to alert any rodent of a human presence but I didn't get the chance today. I'd run out of steam but Miss Cameron hadn't, and was now forging ahead.

'Sometimes I've met rats here,' she mused. 'Nasty little things. I don't know how often we've contacted the sanitary inspector about them, but they keep coming back. The ideal thing of course would be to re-house the family, but Mrs Henderson says she likes it here.' Miss Cameron shrugged. 'Makes you wonder, but who are we to judge?'

She was about to knock on the door when it was pulled open.

'I heard you coming,' said Hilda. A blindingly white nylon overall replaced her crossover pinafore, the rollers and headsquare had been jettisoned to allow the rare sighting of peroxide curls. Even her voice had changed. Had it not been for the missing front tooth, I might not have recognised her.

'Miss Cameron!' She all but curtseyed. 'May wurrd. How naice. Come this way.'

We trooped after her into the bedroom, where a fire blazed and

Mrs Henderson was sitting up looking cheerful, if unfamiliar, with teeth I didn't know she possessed.

Miss Cameron sat on an armchair, I supposed taken from another room and in her honour. She said, 'Just you carry on, Nurse Macpherson. Mrs Henderson and I have a lot to catch up on.' Beaming, she continued, 'And I must say, my old friend, you're looking especially well. Wearing your hair with that band suits you.'

'Nurse Macpherson got it for me.' As my patient pulled on her red winceyette pyjamas, she added, 'Suggested these too. They're much easier to put on than a nightie and they're warm, so that saves the coal. Thrift, eh, Miss Cameron? We know what that is, don't we?'

'Yes – the younger generation have a lot to learn,' Miss Cameron was plainly having a lovely time but my patient's loyalty was undiminished.

She said, 'Well, that's so, but we've to move with the times too. And I must say, we're enjoying Nurse Macpherson's company. We love her bright chat, don't we, Hilda?' But the home help had gone, saying we'd want privacy.

Now, instead of her eagle eye and gossip, I'd an examining tutor. I'd also two thick fresh towels, face cloths, new lavender-scented soap and a basin with the price ticket still attached. Carrying out general nursing care today had become a bit surreal, with my patient so bent on extolling my virtues I nearly gagged her with one of the spare face cloths. Eventually, running out of steam, she turned a bright gaze on the tutor.

'Miss Cameron, d'you ever listen to Nina Simone?'

'I've heard the students speak about her, but no.' If I hadn't associated the tutor with old-fashioned inclinations, I'd have sworn she sounded wistful. 'They say she's a wonderful performer, but I missed out on getting a ticket when she was here recently. How d'you know about her?'

With the air of a conjuror, Mrs Henderson pointed to the radiogram. 'We've got her in there and now that Nurse's finished giving me that lovely wash, she'll put her on.'

'I'll leave you to it whilst I tidy things away,' I said as Nina cranked up and her sounds filled the room. Miss Cameron had been perched on her chair as if listening to a sermon, but by the time I'd returned, she was settled in the chair gazing into the fire, apparently lost in a reverie.

A small hand conducted over the counterpane whilst in the distance Hilda warbled with heart-felt conviction, 'I put a spell on yooou.'

When the LP finished, Miss Cameron stood up, stretched and dropped her shoulders. A dimple appeared. Her voice was even softer than usual as she said, 'I know the students think I'm an old fuddy-duddy and I've always thought The Beatles and Rolling Stones made an awful racket, but d'you know, I must get that record.'

Then she patted Mrs Henderson on the shoulder. 'Thank you, as ever. I can't think of a better place for my students to come for their training and I can see you've made a great bond with this one. Now come along, Nurse, we really must go.'

Following her out, I noticed her step was light and her bum had a slight wiggle, making the skirt box-pleats give a particular swing. Maybe she was remembering wearing a kilt and Highland dancing, but I prefer to think that Miss Cameron was getting in the groove.

27

CATCHING UP

Miss Cameron practically skipped into the classroom. Maybe it was because it was our last day and she'd be getting a break, or maybe she'd good news about our exams.

I glanced over at the castle which, in a fine drizzle, looked particularly indomitable and impregnable. The view made me think of an Edinburgh which wore history like fancy-dress, and having found it fitted, kept it on. Right now, however, the future was more important, with our tutor holding the key to it.

She cleared her throat, checked her skirt's box-pleats were in place, paused as she adjusted her spectacles, then smiled.

'I'm delighted to tell you that you've all passed the exam.' She allowed the class a small buzz of self-congratulation before continuing, 'So now you'll be heading to your own districts where, I trust, you'll remember all we've taught you. For me, anyway, it's been an enjoyable experience although,' she scratched the back of her neck, 'I've a slight concern you might find it strange working on your own without the back-up you've had here. I'm guessing you're going to miss that – for a while anyway.'

Without any practice, we chorused, 'Of course. And you too.' Our shy, modest, serious little tutor deserved respect. We weren't being craven. What class wouldn't be influenced by a dedication shown at every tutorial, or passion for delivery of compassionate professional care?

She cocked her head. 'Actually, I'll probably see most of you from time to time as all but you, Nurse Macpherson, are going to work near here.' She pulled herself up to her full five-foot height. 'So, girls, do remember I'm always here and happy to help with any problems you might have.' She considered me for a moment. 'Of course, I know you can't do that, but I understand Ross-shire has a splendid network of nurses and,' she pursed her lips for a moment before adding, 'Miss MacLeod is a very modern thinker.'

An open file lay on the table. It was there each time we reported on our visits to her and was presumably a record of our own work. She glanced over it, nodded, then closed it with something of a flourish. Giving it a final tap, she said, 'There! You know you've been lucky. You are the last Queen's qualifying nurses that I'll be tutoring.' She altered her tone slightly. 'I can't think that the content of the next course will be very different, but it won't be graced with the Queen's name. So, you be proud of your qualification and its name, and good luck.'

It was good to be back in Ross-shire, but I was struck by the irony of douce Miss Cameron choosing to live in Scotland's busy capital whilst trendy Miss Macleod stayed in quiet Dingwall, where I was now heading.

On the day of my return to Conon Bridge, she'd left a message on my answering machine. 'Welcome back and congratulations, Sister Macpherson. Miss Cameron tells me that you've passed the course. I look forward to seeing you at tomorrow's staff meeting and if you want to use your own car, that's fine. Dr Duncan and I have decided that anybody wanting to use their own transport can now do so.'

Fortrose wasn't mentioned. Maybe Miss Cameron had made a

mistake. I hadn't liked to pursue the matter because she'd blushed as soon as she'd said it. Anyway, Miss Campbell was prone to that, and as I was in the middle of my practical exam, there were other things to think about. Afterwards there never seemed a chance to find out more.

Still, I'd love the chance to work there. 'Suit you very nicely.' I was sure I remembered Miss Cameron saying that.

I'd seen Fortrose and had been beguiled by the little town's simple layout, shops and sturdily-built houses. There was an ancient cathedral near the High Street. Only a fraction of it remained but its red sandstone spoke of another time, long before the Victorian houses fronting the main road were built. The nearby sea gave the air a taste of salt and iodine, whilst the clear high call of gulls above the harbour sang in my ears long after I drove back to my Conon Bridge home. I wondered was it likely to remain that.

Three months away from Ross-shire didn't seem very long, but in that time, spring had called, breathed new life into the countryside, left the larch, rowan, wild cherry and birch trees clad in green and then made way for early summer. The gorse bushes painting the road verge in gold splashes owed their ripening colour to it, and it gave a perfect day.

'Gorse is a terrible plant,' my old crofting friend Mr Munro had once told me. 'There's no feeding in it and the prickles give sheep Orf . . .' He'd scratched his head, looking for a way to describe the word, then settled for, '. . . Impetigo of the mouth.'

No wonder it was the scourge of crofters struggling to halt its relentless march. Still, I couldn't help but savour the flowers' coconut scent coming through the car's open window. I knew that if Jock had still been employed as a roadman he wouldn't have let the plant grow so prolifically along the road, and I was sure that's why none grew near the Duthie house.

Then I saw the brothers. They were standing outside the hen run, apparently having an amiable conversation with, it had to be, Dally and Dally at their feet. From time to time, the hens would look up enquiringly, as if about to give a considered reply. I had to stop even if it would make me late for Miss Macleod's meeting.

'It's the wee nursie!' Jock gave a welcoming cry and elbowed Willie, who'd immediately dropped his eyes, seemingly fascinated by the ground.

He managed a modest, 'Aye,' before hurrying into the house, followed by a faithful hen. He'd have been quicker had he not been wearing such big wellies. Sound floated through the open door. I wondered if the brothers left their telly on all the time. Was I was hearing the BBC test card music? If so, the Duthies must really like telly!

I must have unnerved Willie. Disappointed, I wandered over to a fenced-off piece of ground and noticed a row of flourishing plants. 'Hey, Jock. I didn't know you were a gardener. I wasn't even aware that you had a garden, but that looks like a great crop of tatties.'

Jock beamed. 'That's Willie's work. He's never been much of a gardener before, but he's been watching Percy Thrower on the telly. As soon as the bonny days came, he's been out making that garden.' Jock drew breath. 'And d'you know, Nursie, he's feeling so much better these days, he's been able to dig out that patch and *now* he's planning growing more – depending on what the gardening manny says.'

I wished I had Mr Thrower's powers, then I could get Willie out of the house again, but I was running out of time so I said how pleased I was to see both brothers. 'Look, I'll need to go, Jock. Give my regards to Willie, will you?'

Jock glanced at the house, sighed, then said, 'I'm coming out to have look at that car of yours. I'm thinking you've a new one.' He went up to it, looked it over carefully and, putting a horny hand on the bonnet, gave it a salutary pat. 'Man! Is that no a daft colour,' he said, grinning at the black hand print he'd left on the Imp's white paintwork.

'Hoy!'

It was Willie. He was going so fast it was a wonder his wellies didn't leave a rubber vapour trail. He was waving with one hand, whilst in the other he held a small cardboard box. 'This is for you, Nursie,' he said breathlessly, handing it over. He wiped his nose on his sleeve, tucked both hands behind his dungaree bib and smiled shyly.

'Aw, Willie!' I opened the box and saw half a dozen shiny brown eggs, the occasional bit of feather stuck to a bit of dirt giving provenance. 'Oh my! These look wonderful.'

'Its no from me. It's from the girls,' he said, and hurried away.

'Aye well, ' said Jock, nodding approvingly, 'don't eat them all at once, Nursie. You were once telling me they could make you explode inside.'

Hurrying now, I put the car's accelerator pedal down. When I reached Dingwall's outskirts, I might have forgotten to take it off, had it not been for a line of eccentric-looking cars pulling aged caravans and coming towards me. Men in rough attire, comfortable with driving in the middle of the road, waved as I pulled in to let them past. Dingwall's tinkers were on the move.

I wondered if the bell-tenters were with them, or had they thrown in their lot with Bell. Sister Shiach might know. Hopefully she'd be at the meeting.

Her new car was. Identified by Jomo peeping out from the driver's window of a large estate, it straddled two of the Headquarter's parking areas. I put the Imp well away from the estate, following the example of other car owners.

I was sure I knew them, but going into the meeting room, I

stopped short. This group of nurses looked different. They wore blue, open-necked dresses, made in a light, easy-care material verging on skimpy. Black shoes were gone, replaced by sandals.

The plastic white detachable collar on my heavy-duty dress made my neck feel sticky and uncomfortable. 'Summer's arrived and you're like a fashion parade,' I said, envying the group's easy attire even if I thought Miss Cameron would have fainted at the hem lengths.

Sister Shiach said, 'Yes, there'll be a new dress for you too. Miss Macleod thought we needed a change of image. Wants to make us feel comfortable as well. Of course, some of us weren't keen at first, but you know how it is with our modern-thinking boss.' She gave a small smile. 'Welcome back. How was Auld Reekie?' She seemed a tad pre-occupied and didn't wait for an answer.

At least the room's seating plan hadn't changed. I took my usual place between Daisy and Ailsa.

'Ah! Modern ways,' mused Daisy, who looked years younger. She looked at her knees as if in surprise that she actually had ones. 'It's easy seen that Miss Macleod hasn't had to bend over to give injections lately.'

Ailsa nudged me and whispered. 'Sshh! Keep it dark. Daisy's so pleased she's able to give them easily now, she's practically signed up to join the local darts team.'

'And what about you, Ailsa?' I asked, 'What's new?'

'Nothing much. Things are pretty much the same as when you left here,' she said carelessly.

Daisy, taking a keen interest in our chat, leant over and said with a twinkle, 'Don't you believe a word of it. She hasn't even bought a car. Not like me!' Daisy was smug, then mischievous. 'But of course she hardly needs one, not when she's got Charlie to ferry her about.'

'The ambulance man?'

Ailsa was deprecating. 'Ach! He's just a friend. Really, Daisy. You're just an old gossip.'

Daisy bridled. 'No, I'm not. Otherwise I wouldn't have to cover such a lot of your Saturdays when you and Charlie go dancing in Strathpeffer.'

'I'm presuming you don't go by ambulance?' I said.

Ailsa poked me. 'Never mind me. I hear there's a vacancy in Fortrose. Would you fancy that?'

I nodded. 'It's been mentioned in despatches but nothing concrete.'

'Leave it to me,' said Ailsa, bobbing her head vigorously. 'But, hey! Here comes the boss. Wonder what new tricks she's got up her sleeve and, pardon the analogy but see her hemline, I bet it's been given another hike.'

'Ah! Sister Macpherson. You're back.' Miss Macleod came into the room. Her welcome, as brief as Sister Shiach's, was nevertheless warm, but she seemed a lot more excited about the contents of the clear polythene bag she was carrying.

'These are disposable syringes,' she said, holding up the bag as if it was a prize exhibit and she was addressing the winners. 'And not only that but we've disposable needles to go with them as well. So today's good news, Sisters, is that there'll be no more complaints about getting painful injections from blunt needles.'

'What a waste!' muttered Daisy.

Miss Macleod was swift. 'No it's not, especially when you consider the expense and trouble having to boil up everything. And then, there's the time you'll save. No, Sister Mackay, I'm afraid you'll just have to accept progress. Like everybody else, you'll just collect your supply at the end of our meeting. I think you'll find this new method will be invaluable.'

Daisy squashed, subject closed, Miss Macleod cleared her throat then continued, 'Now, I've been thinking.'

A small groan swept the room.

'Watch out!' murmured Ailsa, and Daisy clicked her teeth.

Undeterred, Miss Macleod looked round the room and frowned. 'You know, I've often thought that this room's not set up properly. Rows of chairs make it far too formal. Doesn't lead to shared discussion and, as we all know, talking's good.' As complete silence greeted this, she put her hands together as if orchestrating a ceilidh. 'So let's get the chairs in a semi-circle and see if that's any better. I know Sister Shiach's got a case history she'd like to discuss. Once we're organised she can talk about it.'

Concerned eyes took in the sister whose unusual anxiety showed in her worried face and nervous scratching of a dimpled arm. She waited for the noise level of scraping chairs moved by irritated people to stop. Then she went to stand behind her chair and, shaking her head in mock despair, began. 'It's actually more of a brainstorming session. I kinda need a bit of advice. You know, in our line of work, it can be difficult not to judge but I see a pair of my old patients reeling home from the pub every other day.' She looked away, as if picturing the scene. 'They're an old couple and, frankly, have been treating their bodies abysmally all their lives. Yet they seem none the worse for it and actually I don't need to visit them any longer.' She nodded at me. 'Sister Macpherson knows who I mean and, in fact, had quite a part in getting them to operate independently.'

I shifted uncomfortably whilst she deliberated for a moment then added, 'For better or for worse, they do seem happy, and I don't grudge those old rascals their happiness.' She sighed. 'But it seems so unfair that I've got a much younger patient and she and her husband are never going to be able to do that. She's dying of breast cancer.'

She gestured at the window through which the sun streamed as if it would forever. 'On days like this, I find it especially hard dealing with something so tragic. And if that's not bad enough, she's got family. Teenagers, a boy and a girl. Now the thing is, she doesn't want them to know – yet.' She bit her lip. 'Wants things to go on as normal, but the trouble is that I don't think she knows how ill she is and it's beginning to be obvious to me, at least, that she's running out of time.'

'D'you see much of the family?' someone enquired.

'Not really. The kids are at school and when they're at home they kinda hide away. I only know when they're around when I hear them playing pop music in their bedrooms.' She spoke without resentment. 'I suppose that's how teenagers are these days but with the mum not wanting them to know anything I can hardly flush them out of their rooms. To tell you the truth, I'm feeling a bit stumped as to what to do.'

'What about the doctor?'

'She doesn't want him around. Says it will just worry everybody. Of course, I've spoken to him and we've discussed it, but my lady's left it too long for any sort of treatment other than me going in and helping as best I can. You know, the usual. Skin care, plumbing matters, dressing a breast that should have been removed ages ago.'

'And the husband?'

Sister Shiach shook her head, almost in despair. 'He's at work and I'm pretty sure he's not aware of the situation either. You'd think he'd be bound to know but she's cute about keeping things secret. She's moved into the spare bedroom 'cos she says his snoring keeps her awake.' She shrugged. 'And maybe he does, but the trouble is that his wife's kept her cancer a secret for so long that that's now a normal pattern.' She looked round the room. 'So my question is, how I can prepare a family for a sad outcome when my patient isn't ready for it?'

'How long have you known the family?' asked Ailsa.

181

'Since the bairns were little.' The memory seemed to momentarily cheer the sister.

Daisy's kind voice broke in. 'So, knowing you, they'll trust you and that's a great bonus. I've had a few cases a bit like that and they are heartbreaking. Looking back, I've never been sure that I was doing or saying the right thing.' She sounded rueful. 'But I do know, certain times came when it was easier to say particular things and, of course, you will be there for afterwards. That's really important.'

Sister Shiach nodded her head slowly. 'Thanks, Daisy. Yes I suppose I should know that already. It's easy to forget that the right moment will probably come, I've just to remember to look for it.' Looking round the room, she smiled and dropped her shoulders. 'You're right, Miss Macleod. It sometimes does help to talk ourselves.' Looking thoughtful, she sat down.

Miss Macleod nodded approvingly. 'Well, we are human and I'm sure as *Sister* Mackay says, you will have the right answer ready. I'm always aware that amongst my staff someone is likely to be dealing with a tragedy unfolding in a patient's house, and that is hard. I've just been on a management course and one of the points that I thought was particularly relevant was that talking out problems is important.'

She turned to me, 'Now, I don't imagine you'll have had Sister Shiach's particular one during your training, but what about giving us a resumé? Any patient that you'll always remember, for example.'

I didn't have to think hard to say it was Mrs Henderson, but before I could go much further, Ailsa cried, 'I got to know her when I was doing my training, and Hilda, her amazing home help. She couldn't have managed to stay at home without her.'

I hadn't thought of Ann from Muir of Ord as being particularly vocal but now she too spoke. 'Home helps are, to my mind, unsung heroines. My Miss Forbes has had her life transformed by one. The Munros, who are her neighbours, have become involved too. Mr Munro's actually managed to turn her old ratty dog into a nice wee animal. Getting out and about and making him feel useful's given him a new lease of life and he's going to love these disposable syringe-things.'

'So after your Edinburgh adventures, where now?' asked Ailsa. 'Is it back to Conon Bridge doing relief work?' The question was casual.

'I'm not sure,' I hedged.

Miss Macleod looked surprised. 'But surely you're going to Fortrose. I'm sure we talked about it before you went to Edinburgh.'

I was certain that we hadn't, but it would be hard to argue the point, especially with Miss Macleod. There was a short silence before Sister Shiach put in a smooth, 'Yes, talking has its place, but listening's just as important.'

28

ALL CHANGE

I loved the view from my parents' upland Morayshire farm. It extended over the Moray Firth to the Black Isle, and behind that to Ben Wyvis, a huge sprawling mountain further to the north. It dominated the landscape but only if it was a clear day, whilst the Rosemarkie transmitter, even if it was less attractive, was a constant landmark. 'If you keep your eye on that, you might just manage to see me.' I said, getting ready to leave after a few days visiting my folks. 'Pity I can't fly. I'd get to Fortrose in half an hour.'

My father didn't think much of my sense of direction. 'Ach, you'd miss by a mile,' he said, not entirely joking, 'then you'd have to walk at least that distance to get back to your new home town. Better stick to road and ferry.'

Recalling the conversation, I drove to Inverness's Kessock ferry terminal. I saw Munlochy, Daisy's fiefdom just across the water, and wondered if she was on duty or on this side, enjoying newfound mobility in her Mini.

A tall man, with hands like paddles, stood at the ferry ramp, beckoning to the line of waiting cars. The twenty-mile road journey from Inverness to the Black Isle was long compared to the ferry taking the strait between the Beauly and Moray Firths. However, I was about to realise that motorists might have to pay for the shortcut in more ways than just the ferry tariff.

The attendant, a permanent scowl stamped on his craggy features, was signalling to cars with such an impatient gesture I wondered if the firths were running out of water. It was impossible to make eye contact with the man on account of his sea-sprayed spectacles. Still, he must have seen the cars, and even if the drivers couldn't hear him, his gape-mouthed words were plain enough. 'Come on!'

'Come *on!*' His hands picked up speed, which is pretty much what he wanted the drivers to do.

He glared as the queue inched forward. His exasperation grew. Caution seemed to be holding back motorists unwilling to follow his directions. He seemed anxious to cram in as many vehicles as he could whilst the drivers showed a similar concern for not driving over the edge. Eventually the first couple of cars were parked to his specifications but when the drivers came out of their vehicles, they hung, ashen-faced, over the boat side. Maybe, like me, it was their first time on the ferry.

'Come on!'

As I started to crawl forward, something large leapt out of the water. Distracted, I jammed on the brakes to the consternation of the driver behind me and the annoyance of my navigator. He yelled, 'Watch! No! Mind! No! Just forget that bloody porpoise!'

At least it made a change from his 'Come on' cry. I'd soon learn that those beautiful creatures leaping in the firth were everyday sights, but, right now, I had to ignore them. Flustered by a car horn tooting behind and the attendant's gesticulations, I shot forward, making contact with the car's bumper in front.

The attendant nodded approvingly. 'Fine.' He turned to the driver behind me, who'd stalled her engine and couldn't start it again.

His signalling technique didn't work so he stomped to the old grey Hillman Minx, giving its rusting bodywork a sour look. The driver wound down her window. So did I.

I could have sat listening to the slap of water on the boat side, the mewing cry of gulls as they wheeled above the ever-changing colour of sea water and admired the rich green of a peninsula called The Black Isle. I'm ashamed to admit that eavesdropping on what sounded like a lively conversation was far more interesting.

'If you get out, I'll give you a hand to push your old rust-bucket to a parking place,' he said.

She was adamant. 'No! If we do that we could do more damage than it's worth.'

I thought she had a point. A gull landed nearby, adding its squeaking-gate squabble cry to the continuing argument.

Eventually the car door opened and she got out, shouting, 'Well, do it yourself then!'

She was dressed for a Scottish summer in a sensible brown coat, a scarf and a green tartan head square. A sea breeze made the back of it flap behind her like a small windsock as she strode off to join the other travellers at the boat's side. Fascinated, the rest of us watched as the attendant got into the car, slammed the door shut, turned on the engine and moved the car. He did it effortlessly. Unimpressed, the car owner continued to inhale on her cigarette whilst gazing seaward.

I was curious about the woman and wondered if she was a local or someone heading north. But this was my first day in Fortrose, and with other things on my mind, I was keen for the ferry to get going. So too, it seemed, was the attendant, meantime scanning the waiting area and checking his watch. He glanced up at the captain, who was looking out from a control room resembling a turreted telephone kiosk. Both men shrugged, a lever was pushed and slowly the metal-boarding ramp began to rise. Then it stopped as a blue Mini came down the slipway with the roaring sound of a gear stuck in third. With a huge echoing clang, the ramp returned to ground level.

The attendant's face relaxed into a beam. His signalling hand was expansive and transformed into a welcoming gesture as he guided the Mini into a space big enough for an ambulance. As the driver wound down her window, he cried in the cheeriest manner, 'Hello, hello, Sister Mackay. We were thinking you were about to miss the ferry. Dougie-Dog would have had something to say if we hadn't waited, wouldn't he?' He fished in his pocket and handed something in. 'And he'll be looking for his usual, I suppose.'

I was sure Daisy's car would be the first one off and, reluctant to disturb her royal treatment, didn't let her know I was on the ferry. Anyway, it was a very short journey, with most of her time taken up chatting to the attendant. When we reached the other side and she'd been safely seen off, he resumed normal service. Now, forgetting anything other than my own destination, I headed for Fortrose.

My new home was on a road just off the High Street and tucked between two stone-built houses. Mine was white-washed, had small-paned windows and the quaint charm of a gingerbread house. I wasn't expecting visitors but a young couple were waiting in the small garden at the front door. I should have sussed problems but was too excited at arriving to pay much attention to the girl's haunted eyes or his anxious sidelong glances at her. She wore a short-sleeved dress and held up her arm so I could see that it was bandaged.

She spoke apologetically, 'We were on the High Street looking for something for this, but the chemist's closed. Then we came down here and saw the Nursing Sister sign outside your door and thought that you could maybe help.' Fresh blood marked the outside of the bandage, which went from her wrist to her elbow. 'I seem to have hurt myself, haven't I, Johnny?' She looked up at him as if she needed his assurance.

'That's for sure.' He spoke very softly. 'You're always doing that, darling.' He had the bright-eyed, fresh-faced outdoor look that would have earned him a Curly McLain part in *Oklahoma*. She, on the other hand, had the frail look of a piece of thistledown. Her eyes were dark pools sunk in a pinched white face with her mini-dress, its vivid turquoise colour making it even more of a contrast. A small smile flickered across her thin lips, then she grimaced and clutched her arm.

'I'm new. Only just arrived,' I explained, searching for the house key, 'but come in. There's been a relief nurse covering here and Rosemarkie and she's been working from the wee office.' I pointed to a window on the right-hand side of the house. 'I'm sure we'll find something for your arm there. You didn't think to go to the doctor?'

The girl began to pull on some strands of her long lank hair as she said, 'No, we were just passing through. Johnny's the one who's anxious. Not me. Not really.'

She followed me into the house, calling over her shoulder, 'You should stay outside, Johnny. You're that big I don't think there'll be room for you. Anyway, you don't like the sight of blood.'

Johnny seemed relieved. 'Good idea, Lorn, but maybe as the lassie says, we should take you to a doc. You can see she's just moving in.'

Lorn came back sharp. 'No! I'm sure that I'll be fine. The nurse here'll sort me. It's just a wee thing.'

'Oh well, if you're sure. You're so brave you make me feel a right Jessie.' He sounded forlorn.

Lorn took a seat in the office. 'Men!' she shrugged, then started to look about the small room with a lively interest.

'I think he's just concerned about you, Lorn. Now let's have a look at this arm. What have you done to it?'

It was a general question but her answer was almost defensive.

'A careless mistake with broken glass.' She patted her hair. As she sat back, she looked about her again.

The office wasn't designed as a casualty outlet but it had a small instrument steriliser, wash hand basin and enough room to set out the wound-cleaning equipment I found stored in a cupboard. I unwound the bandage, aware of her eyes trained on my reaction.

'Did you nick your finger?' I asked, puzzled by fresh blood on the outside of the crepe bandage when the actual wound looked as it was an old, if neglected, one.

'No.' Lorn shook her head violently. She sucked her finger and casually slipped that hand into her dress's deep pockets. 'I don't know how that got there. But look, it's fine. Really.' She jumped up.

I put out a soothing hand. 'No it's not. Just you sit down. You've got a nasty sore there and it does need looking at but, you know, I think it would be better without such bulky dressing.' My finger traced an irritated area of skin round a straight gash on her forearm. 'Sometimes too much bandaging can encourage infection.'

'Infection?' She jumped at the word.

'Well, maybe that's too strong a word. Tenderness – that's probably a better one. But actually, the wound needs a little soothing care and, you'll see, it'll soon clear up with that.' As I got busy with antiseptic lotions, Lorn, conspicuously averting her gaze, looked out of the window. 'Honestly, Johnny's such a fuss,' she said, watching her boyfriend, who was pacing outside like an expectant father.

'He really cares for you,' I said, 'and he'll be pleased you can tell him your arm isn't going to fall off.'

Lorn merely chewed on a lock of hair. When I was finished, she got back to Johnny, holding up the dressed arm like a torchbearer. 'Look! I'm ready to go home now.'

'Great! And has she to do anything more to it, Nurse?'

'I think it'll heal fine if it's kept clean and dry. And why not visit your own nurse or doctor? Where was it you said you stayed?'

But they were already halfway along the street with Lorn seeming to force the pace. Moving out of the reach of Johnny's arm, she called back, 'Thanks, we'll come and visit you when you've more time. See how you're settling in.'

As I started to clear away the equipment I thought about Lorn and Johnny and wished that I didn't feel so uneasy about them. Maybe knowing more about them would have helped me explain better to Lorn how easy it was to get her arm to heal. It only needed simple care, but somehow I wasn't convinced she'd listen.

Since I wasn't really open for business and not expecting any other callers, I finished clearing away. I was about to start moving my belongings in when there was such a sharp rap on the window. I nearly dropped the newly sterilised forceps. I was sure I didn't know anybody in Fortrose, but immediately recognised my caller in her tartan headsquare.

29

A DAY TO REMEMBER!

'Sorry, lassie, I know you've just arrived.' The woman was as breathless as she was apologetic. 'And I won't take up your time.' She held up a thermos flask. 'I thought I'd bring you something to oil the flitting wheels.'

She was so friendly and had such a touch of mischief, I got cheeky. 'I think that if there's anything needing oiled it's that car of yours.'

She laughed, lines etching deep into her brown face. 'Blast! I wondered if you'd heard that exchange. Yes, I did see you. You'll soon find that there's no secrets in Fortrose and even less on that ferry. I'm sorry, you didn't see me in my finest hour, but the ticket bloke's so sour you'd think he lived on lemons. By the way, I'm Molly.' Her handshake was brisk. My hand came back feeling slightly earthy. I noticed her grimed nails and wondered if she was a gardener.

I opened the door wide. 'You must come in. Do, please.'

'No, no. I can see you need to get on, but maybe when you've a minute you could call in to our house – we're just down the road from you. We've a lassie staying with us at the moment. Single girlie. We're looking after her, you see, but she's as scared of her family finding out,' she tapped the middle button of her coat and raised her eyebrows, 'as she is of being seen by a medical cove, but

I know she needs a look, if only for myself and the Rev's sake.' Molly narrowed her eyes in thought and turned on her heel. 'Nothing dramatic, you understand, it's Nature, after all.'

'What's your address?'

She tied her head square so tightly it gave her a double chin. 'Church of Scotland Manse. You'll easy find it. Now I must dash, otherwise I might get an urge to help you settle in and you look as if you can manage perfectly well yourself.' She searched in her pocket, found a packet of fags, offered me one.

'No?' Casting her eyes heavenward, as if in pity, she lit one, inhaling on it with deep satisfaction. Then, in a cloud of smoke, she was gone. I was disappointed. I'd no sooner arrived and met people than they seemed in a hurry to leave. Maybe I should go and say hello to the local doctor before he disappeared as well.

It was late afternoon when I drove through Rosemarkie, the picturesque village half a mile from Fortrose and also part of my district.

'There's no big hurry to visit old Mrs Reid,' Dr Jack had said. 'She lives in a wee wooden house on the Rosemarkie to Cromarty road. You should find her easily enough, although whether she lets you in or not is quite another matter.' He sucked his lip in frustration. 'She showed me the door the last time I called.' He tapped his head. 'I think things might be going a little awry there. She's got a schizophrenic history and it's starting to look as if she's neglecting herself and her cats as well. That good Samaritan Molly kind of keeps an eye on her, minds her garden, but there's only so much she can do. Anyway, Molly's a gardener, not a nurse.' His lips twitched, then he continued, 'so it'd be good to get your opinion. With a bit of luck, she'll allow you to see her.'

Thinking of Miss Forbes and LBP's uncertain temper, I asked, 'Has she a dog?'

He might have thought it was an odd question, but he took it in his stride. 'No, her cats are enough.' He'd the pleasant unruffled manner of an experienced GP but I could see he was busy. It'd be a good start if I could prove how useful I was.

Mrs Reid's house was easy to find once I forgot about the picturesque aspect of the drive and concentrated on staying on the road. Even though the doctor had mentioned Molly's expertise, I was still surprised to see such a well-tended garden. Rows of vegetables flourished in a fenced-off area, marigolds made a bright and cheerful statement in a flower pot on one side of the front door, whilst a clump of cat mint grew on the other.

'Hi Puss,' I said to the tortoise-shell-coloured cat sunning herself in the middle of it. 'You'd better not let Molly catch you doing that.'

By way of answer, the cat arched her back, spat and ran to the back of the house, bushy tail streaming behind her.

'Hello.' I knocked at the door, but got no reply. Carefully, I tried the handle. The door was locked. I tried again, then peeped through the letterbox. An awful smell came through, as well as some faint noises. I tried to picture the scene inside and prayed that if it came to the worst, the smell was only dead cat.

There were windows, one at either side of the door, with half-drawn curtains over them. These so limited the view into two rooms that all I could see were furniture-crowded, dark, dingy-looking places, but no Mrs Reid.

Hurrying now, I took the cracked paving slabs leading round to the back, only to find the door here locked as well. However, there were a couple of windows, set out much the same as the front, but those had half-net screens, and they allowed a better view into two other rooms. The first one had to be the kitchen with its oilcloth-covered table with a pot of porridge sitting on top and a mangy-looking black cat licking out of it. With that certain arrogance cats have when safely out of reach and intending to stay put, it looked up, flicked its tail, and continued eating.

But at least there wasn't a body. Maybe Mrs Reid was out for the day. Buying a lovely ribbon perhaps in that nice haberdashery store I'd spotted in Fortrose. A slight breeze made the surrounding trees sigh as if at such a silly thought, and I went back to thinking that I'd done everything with nothing needing to be fixed.

The sun glanced through the tree branches, making shadows of them on the ground. I stepped over them on my way to the last window. Thinking more kindly of my nice new home comforts than the bed of nettles meantime embracing my ankles, I peered through the grimy cobwebbed glass.

I'd have been seriously spooked if it had been dark. It was bad enough on a sunlit late afternoon with the nearby fir trees whispering amongst themselves, the quick repeated *chink-chink* alarm call of a blackbird sending out a cat warning, to look in and see a scene that was reminiscent of Miss Havisham in her final days.

An old woman with long straggling white hair lay, surely unconscious, in a huge old-fashioned bed covered in a red satin quilt. Its grandeur was as much at odds with the shabby room as were the other occupants. Kittens. As far as was discernible, Mrs Reid was surrounded by them. I took a deep breath, blinked, cleaned the window and looked harder. I'd to be glad that at least she was alive, even if her respirations were so laboured they shifted the bed-covering and made the animals look as if they were surfing on a crimson sea.

It was useless knocking on the window. I tried, then had a go at opening it. Got nowhere. I ran back to the kitchen window. It wouldn't budge. The cat continued eating. I heaved hard and managed to ease open a small gap. Then adrenaline came to my aid. Between that and muscle, I managed to yank up the window, ignoring its scream of protest.

No thanks to the constricting limitations of the new uniform, I bundled through the gap. My hand landed in the porridge pot, the cat scratched my leg.

Drat! A ladder! I could feel it running up my leg. I wasn't in the mood to be grateful it wasn't a mouse. Not with that hungry assailant. She'd scarpered and was now green-eyed, spitting and glaring out from under a rocking chair.

The house felt cold with the kitchen range fire long dead. The smell of ammonia was eye-watering in an atmosphere of quiet despair. The only thing to bring it alive would be sunshine and fresh air, but Mrs Reid would surely need a lot more than that.

'Mrs Reid?'

I hadn't really expected a reply but neither had I anticipated the grotesque accompaniment to my patient's heavy rasping breath. Five purring kittens were cosily arranged round the old lady. It was awful the way they'd sought comfort and warmth, and found it beside a seriously ill human being. With matter in their eyes, they didn't look that healthy themselves and they were pitifully thin, as was she.

Tiny and old, she was burning up. Her skin was dry, there was a worrying flush on her cheeks and her weak pulse was racing. I didn't need to take her temperature to know it was at danger point. She was so deeply unconscious the only perceptible response was that when I lifted one of her eyelids, the pupil dilated.

The room was airless and dusty, but the animals were completely at home. I supposed the porridge-eating cat must be the kittens' mother and used to a least one human being. The tiny animals kept on purring as I tried to figure out what to do first. Struck by the irony of this being almost a summer equivalent of Willie with his hypothermia and the problem of getting his low temperature up, I was now faced with the challenge of getting this patient's high one down. I picked up a thick empty glass off the floor, dumped out the dead fly and ran back to the kitchen.

Had my Edinburgh Mrs Collins been here, I thought as I filled the tumbler with water, she'd have had the sink's brass taps polished and she'd have been horrified at the pile of dirty dishes filling the wooden draining board. She certainly wouldn't have approved of using water in the way I was about to.

I sprinkled some on Mrs Reid's forehead. The kittens blinked and stopped purring. One shook its head as if bewildered, and since I couldn't immediately think what to do with such vulnerable animals, I left them where they were. I also figured if they were moved I might have to add an angry cat to the problems list.

A telephone would be a godsend though it was doubtful that my patient had one. Heart pounding, I raced back to the living area and cast round desperately. Nothing. I'd no option other than leaving the house to get help. At least I'd get one door open, and since I knew she had to have medical help, the front one would be the handiest. As I hurried along the corridor leading to it, I spotted a brown plaited cable on the skirting board. Telephone cable! It led from a connection point beside the door to one of the front rooms I'd tried to look into from outside.

Now that I was actually in it and despite all the furniture clutter and jumble in the room, I got to the empty display cabinet at the far end of the room easily enough. It had two wally dugs on its top, as if guarding the black Bakelite telephone sitting between them. I couldn't imagine why it was in such an awkward place, or even that the GPO was still servicing the line.

Praying for the miracle of a dialling tone, I reached for the receiver.

30

A RESCUE PARTY

Dr Jack's wife answered the phone, unaware that I considered the sound of any voice at the end of the line miraculous. After I explained the reason for the call, she was calm, just as Dr Jack had promised. 'As well as looking after the family, my wife takes the calls if I'm not around. She's my right-hand woman,' he'd explained when I asked what was the best way for us to communicate. 'So you can call any time.' He'd sounded proud.

He'd good reason. Mrs Jack had such a matter-of-fact way, combined with a voice as soothing as honey, that I felt I already knew her, and she certainly knew Mrs Reid.

'Gosh!' she said, 'it didn't take you long to drum up some business. It's a good thing you've our telephone number, though we didn't think you'd need it so soon. Unfortunately my husband's out at the moment, but he'll be home shortly.'

'Mrs Reid needs to go to hospital. Both her condition and her home situation's dire.' I hoped not to sound as panicky as I felt.

'Yes, that's always been a bit dodgy. My husband's hinted as much and I'm sure he'll trust your judgement. It's just a pity we've had to wait for an emergency before doing anything about the poor woman.' Her tone lightened. 'Anyway, I'll get in touch with the Ross Memorial and let them know to expect Mrs Reid. I'm pretty sure they already know her. You make a 999 call for an ambulance and as soon as he's home, the doctor can call the hospital with the details. Sounds like she's got pneumonia from what you're saying.'

Gosh! A diagnosis! And probably an accurate one. My respect for Mrs Jack was complete.

She continued, 'You'll manage to go with her in the ambulance?'

'Uh huh. If we can get the doors unlocked to get her out of the house. If not, we might have to squeeze her through the window that I came in.'

'You sound in control,' she said, laughing, then just before putting down the phone, added, 'In the meantime I'll think of some solution to those blessed cats.'

The black one had already decided its future, shooting outside as soon as I unlocked the door and opened it. It gave a brief backward look, reminiscent of blowing a raspberry, then disappeared. I wondered where to put her young so that she would come back to resume her maternal duties.

Little could be done about the house's squalid condition, but at least there was fresh air coming in through the open door. Mrs Reid was so vulnerable I only wanted an ambulance man able to deal with the present emergency. The state of the house was incidental, but it would be helpful if he'd a strong stomach and a poor sense of smell.

The phone rang. It was so unexpected it gave me a fright.

Molly's breathless voice came over. 'Hello, lassie! Mrs Jack's just been telling me about Mrs Reid. Heavens above! I've been so caught up with our girlie that I haven't been out to see Mrs Reid for ages.' She clicked her tongue as if annoyed at herself, then resumed, 'Now I don't want to interfere but I'm coming right over with some toiletries. I'll bet she hasn't got any. She'll get clothes from the hospital so their laundry can take care of all that. And that's a bonus. I'm sure she won't have anything decent to wear herself.'

She gave a phlegmy cough. 'And don't worry about the cats. There's kittens too? See if you can find space in a drawer and pop them in there. That should do in the meantime.' With a warning remark about fleas, she finished the call.

Despite everything, I had to smile. Fleas? Make my day! I hadn't spotted any bite marks on Mrs Reid, but those kittens needed moving *now*. Molly's suggestion made sense. There was a small chest in the bedroom under a pile of junk. Despite the missing knobs, I managed to pull out the bottom drawer, which with its assortment of old matted woollen jerseys made for a perfect bijou residence. The kittens took to it with the helpless trust of small dependent animals. Uttering small cries, they moved close in to snuggle against one another. The mother must have heard them because she appeared at the bedroom door, stalked past me and jumped in beside them. With calls of delight, the kittens plugged in.

'To the manor born, Puss?' I said, wondering where cats fitted into standard practice nursing care. What would Miss Cameron say? More importantly, I was sure that Mrs Jack's diagnosis was correct. Without the kittens I could now concentrate on getting Mrs Reid in a sitting-up position. That should help her congested lungs to expand. She was so light it was easy to get her upright, and staying that way, with some supportive old cushions that had been lying on the floor.

'This should help you.' I knew that even if she couldn't speak, it didn't mean she couldn't hear or be aware of her surroundings. Now that I could see her better, it seemed more natural talking to her as well.

Her tiny face had ingrained dirt marking its many lines, her cheeks were sunken and whatever personalities dominated her schizophrenic brain, none looked out from behind those faded, dead-looking eyes. I imagined that her hair would be really white if washed free of soot. Surely she hadn't thought that she was a chimney sweep!

'I think you've been up the lum.' I wiped her face with a damp face cloth. 'I thought this was an old bit of cardboard until it was thrown into water, and I'm sorry but I couldn't find a towel. Actually, my dear, you're so like a wee hot stove you'll soon dry off.' I lifted up one of her skeletal-looking arms and popped a thermometer under it. 'Let's see what your temperature says.'

Regardless of being sponged, new air circulating about her and freedom from the quilt and kittens, Mrs Reid's temperature was still going up. Her breathing was getting more laboured and she began to mutter in delirium. Hearing her disturbed babble, the black cat shot an anxious glance over the top of the drawer.

'Don't bother looking like that,' I said, temper fraying, 'you must know this is a bit of an emergency. If there's any more of that bad language I'll shut you and your family into that bloomin' drawer and throw away the key.'

The cat yawned, began to clean her face, then stopped, listening. She might have been alarmed but I was delighted by the sound of a vehicle drawing up outside the house. Right after it came the roar of a car which must have had a hole in its exhaust pipe.

The sound of more slamming doors and people greeting each other made a noise like a cheery bus party pulling in for a cup of tea. Somebody coughed. It had to be Molly.

'Hello, hello!'

I recognised Charlie's voice. I'd forgotten he might be the ambulance driver, but as soon as I saw him coming into the room I remembered his bright optimistic way. His Beatles haircut was new.

'Taxi!'

He'd brought a stretcher. I don't know why I was worried about anybody noticing or being affected by my patient's surroundings because Charlie just got to work. 'Right, Sister, you roll her over and I'll slide in the stretcher canvas.'

It was pathetically easy to get our patient's bird-like form out to the ambulance where Molly was waiting. She waved a toilet bag. 'I'll stick this in the front and after you've gone, I'll round up the cats and shut the house.'

As we lifted Mrs Reid into the ambulance, her breathing changed. It sounded horribly like a death rattle, but Charlie was unfazed. 'Just as well I checked the oxygen cylinder was full.' He seemed far more anxious when he said, 'But, Sister, you're not going to be sick, are you?'

'Certainly not! But let's get going.'

'You'd have been glad to get that lady into hospital,' said Charlie as he drove the ambulance back out of the hospital car park and turned towards the town.

'I certainly am, and thank goodness for a staff that takes the admission of someone in thick pink knickers and a tea-stained vest in their stride.'

Charlie laughed. 'I bet they've seen some sights. Part of the job, I suppose, but at least they knew we were coming and were ready for her. Whoops!' He jammed on the brakes, just managing to avoid running over two small children who'd been pushing each other off the kerbside.

There was a small, slight figure I didn't recognise standing beside a familiar one wearing gold earrings glinting in jet black hair. As she grabbed the children, she swiped each one with a practised hand.

'Ye silly wee limmers!' Bell McGlone's words floated melli-fluously through the evening air.

Charlie took a deep breath, shook his head and waved a finger, to which one child responded by sticking out her tongue. The other, who had a scarred face, followed suit.

I'd forgotten to ask Sister Shiach about the bell-tenters, but watching the little group heading off with the women shaking their heads and the children laughing, I reckoned they looked very much at home.

31

NOT QUITE ALL
IN A DAY'S WORK

It had been a long day but I didn't particularly want to go home. I'd been in Fortrose for over month and Lorn and Johnny, the odd couple whom I'd met on my first day, had taken to regularly dropping by in time to catch me the minute I'd finished work. From their old pick-up parked outside my door, their eager, anxious faces would look out at me with such pathetic enthusiasm that, torn between guilt and exasperation, I'd invite them into the house.

Lorn would get out and, pulling Johnny behind her, she'd tug her hair a little, taking the usual line of, 'We're a bit bored and thought that, seeing as you're still new here, you might fancy a bit of company. And you're such a laugh. You always cheer us up. Anyway, we fancied a cup of tea.'

I'd usually ask about her arm, noticing that she wore long sleeves all the time now, but she always made light of it. Said it was better. A cup of tea and a chat – now that was far more important.

The pair seemed happy to sit in my snug little sitting room, skilfully fending off personal questions whilst smoothly finding out about my life.

One evening Lorn said, 'It must be lonely here on your own.' She twiddled her hair. 'I bet you've a boyfriend tucked away somewhere that you're not telling anybody about.'

I thought about David. Our brief encounter in Edinburgh hadn't completely soured our relationship and we'd kept in touch, spasmodically.

'Well, there is somebody, but he's just a friend.' Even if I was pleased, I aimed for a careless tone. 'He used to live in Glasgow but he's just written to say that he'll be coming home to look after his father's hotel in Forres.'

'Just across the water from here then,' said Johnny with a twinkle. 'And certainly handier to get to than Glasgow.'

'And what about yourselves?' I asked, seizing a chance to find out a little more about the couple. 'I guess you two live near here as well.'

Apparently Lorn kept house for Johnny, who was a farm labourer near Fearn. She gave the impression that her housekeeping skills weren't wonderful. As time went past, I was beginning to find it getting harder to keep encouraging someone convinced she'd never improve.

I sighed. Today had already been hard going.

I hadn't quite been introduced to the pupils of a local primary school as the nit nurse but the elderly schoolmistress would have preferred that to the alternative, I tried to tactfully suggest. Pursing her lips, she said, 'Sister indeed! Our last nurse was very happy just being called Nurse. But if that's the way you like to be addressed, then that's the way I suppose I'll have to do it.' She turned to her pupils. 'Now, children, you remember our last nurse?'

'Yes, Miss.'

'Well, this is our new one, but she wants to be called *Sister* instead. Fancy!'

The children, with an aptitude the teacher might have appreciated better spent on their times table, immediately picked up on her annoyance. Lining up to show their nails, teeth and hair, a chant began. "Oooh, she wants to be called Sister. F-a-a-a-n-c-e-e." The teacher, apparently deaf, looked out of the window.

I looked at the sniggering, pushing and shoving queue. 'Before I start,' I said, 'I'd like to show you something.'

I went to the blackboard and picked up a piece of chalk. 'May I?'

I didn't wait for the teacher's answer. 'Now, listen,' I began. 'Here's a secret. I'm not only a sister but I'm a hunter . . . of these.' I drew a picture of a louse. 'That's what I'll be looking for.'

'But that's a crab!' scoffed someone.

'Very good. And yes, it's certainly like one. But this is tiny, got more legs and it starts off life as an egg. A louse loves laying ones in human hair, where they can hatch.' I tapped my head all over in a light way, hoping to illustrate the flight path of a louse. 'And hopefully I won't see any in yours, 'cos all of that action can make your head feel very scratchy.'

'Yuck!' said a small child. 'I'm feeling sick.'

'Rubbish!' said the teacher, looking at her watch. 'We must thank Sister Macpherson for that little lecture but I'm sure she'd like to get on.'

'Just one more thing,' I said, now rather enjoying myself and catching the teacher having a furtive scratch herself. 'Brushing your hair's great. Apparently it breaks the lice's legs.'

'Would there be blood?' someone wondered aloud.

'I expect so, but I've never actually seen that,' I had to admit, 'but maybe that's because all the children I've seen wash their hair and, of course, brush, brush, brush it.'

'Brush, brush, bru-sh-it!' chanted the children, sliding the last two words together in gleeful harmony.

I'd ended the session issuing each child with a 'just in case' bottle of nit-deterring shampoo.

'Maybe you should have one too,' I said, handing one to the teacher. 'Apparently lice prefer laying their eggs in clean hair.'

As I turned into my street, my heart sank at seeing the now familiar sight of the pick-up truck parked outside the house. On the other hand, I was always delighted to see Molly, especially now. Taking shameful delaying tactics, I was happy to stop as she flagged me down at the manse gate. I wound down the window and she leant in, a big smile lighting her face.

'I've great news, lassie,' she said. 'Our young friend who's been staying with us has gone home to her mum and dad to have her baby, and d'you know this? They actually want her to keep it.' She shook her head in disbelief. 'Now that is a miracle!' Her tone implied surprise at such a thing. Then she continued, 'And, of course, we'll be keeping in touch so she knows we're here for her too.'

I thought about the young unmarried girl who'd sought succour under the manse roof. She'd arrived in Fortrose about the same time as myself and had been both in denial and despair at her situation, and telling no one but Molly and her husband.

Still, it had been easy enough for me to visit the manse. Then I was able to keep a discreet eye on her, whilst keeping Molly up-to-date with news about Mrs Reid.

'The hospital says she's improving and putting on weight – a bit like her cats,' I'd said one day, nodding at the sleek and well-fed brood Molly was now caring for with the same generosity of spirit she was giving the young lass.

I might have said the same to her, but I'd to wait for her to acknowledge her pregnancy to me first. Then, one day when watching the cat attend to her kittens, she suddenly burst out. 'I envy that cat. She's just doing what a mother does.' Between tears she went on, 'But I know my family would never forgive me for having a baby out of wedlock.'

This had to be the green light. At least I could start a dialogue, which included giving her ante-natal care. From my cursory glances at her beforehand, I could see she was keeping well enough, but still refusing to see any doctor was a worry. Patient confidentiality was one thing but as the time passed and with her pregnancy making more demands on her body, I knew she should have blood tests that I couldn't do and vitamin B_9 (folic acid) tablets only a doctor could prescribe.

Thinking about the girl and the surprise of her return home, I leant back in the car seat, savouring the moment. I said, 'Now that is good news, and Molly, I suspect you're responsible for this miracle.'

'No, no!' She waved a dismissive hand. 'My husband knows more about that sort of thing and his pastoral care was crucial. Once he'd a chat with her and she allowed us to approach her parents, the rest was easy. Things happened very quickly. Now, lassie,' she tapped me gently on the arm, 'you go and get your feet up. You look tired.'

It was such a perfect summer's evening Molly had even jettisoned her coat and headsquare.

'That looks remarkably like a twin-set. Pale green suits you. Are you going somewhere nice?'

'The Women's Guild have a meeting tonight and I'm hoping that between them and the vet we'll find homes for all the cats,' she said. 'Even if the manse is a barn of a place, the minister's beginning to protest at so many of them.'

'So it'll no longer be a case of the minister's cats then?' I was laughing now. Molly's brisk take on life always made me feel better.

As it was such a pleasant evening, I could maybe prise my guests off their beloved sofa and get them to sit outside. I'd buy them a fish and chip supper from the cheerful Italians round the corner and we could eat them in my sheltered little garden at the back of the house.

Johnny came out of his pick-up van as soon as he saw me. He looked distracted.

'I'm not staying.' The words came tumbling out. 'Lorn's in hospital. She went last night. I had to take her, Sister.' He buried his face in his hands. 'It was awful. I've never seen so much blood. It was everywhere.'

I was too shocked to say anything. Only the call of a gull setting up the chorus of others filled the silence between us. Johnny took a huge sighing breath then continued, 'I knew there was something no right but I never thought she'd try and take her life.'

'Was it Raigmore you took her?' It was all I could think to say.

'Aye.' Johnny looked around before he whispered, 'But she's been transferred to Craig Dunain.' He said it as if the name of the Inverness psychiatric hospital was a disease in itself.

Once I'd taken him into the house and calmed him as best I could, Johnny went on. 'She was awful bad-used when she was a bairn. She was in a foster home with others and it was a terrible place. She wouldn't speak about it much but when she did, I'd see the bandage back on her arm afterwards.'

'You're not to blame,' I said. 'Look! I'm a nurse and I should have spotted something was wrong. I knew she wasn't happy but it never dawned on me that she would be so completely depressed. Have you heard how she is now?'

'Well, she's alive and the hospital says that physically she'll soon get better.' Johnny lifted his head and spoke in a broken voice, 'But to tell you the truth, I've had enough. I was never able to make her happy and I know I never will. Anyway, she says she doesn't want to see anybody but you.'

'Me?' I was astonished.

'Yes, says you're her best friend.' He rose and put out his hand.

'I'm not having her back with me so, if you do go and see her, will you tell her that?'

'Johnny—'

I tried to stop him, but he was already out the door and climbing into his truck. With a tentative wave of his hand, he was gone.

32

LOOKING FORWARD

Craig Dunain Hospital was built in days when it was all right to call it a lunatic asylum. In 1969, vestiges of a grim past still remained, with Victorian turrets, towers and mean-looking windows making the hospital look like something out of a gothic horror movie. The surrounding grounds, however, were attractive and well-tended, and I wondered if the people I saw working in them were patients. Whoever they were, they were totally absorbed in their work, and doing a good job.

Following directions to Lorn's ward, I walked along a corridor where highly polished floor surfaces spoke of hard labour. Had the wood panelled walls been capable of words, I imagined they'd have told dark stories.

I was so lost in the past that for a split second I imagined a ghost was coming towards me.

'Ah, Mrs Reid!' A nurse came flying out of a ward. 'You wee rascal. How did you get out?'

Without the name, I might not have recognised the little sprite with the scrubbed face and pure white hair. She was wearing a towelled striped dressing gown. Only the fact that it swamped her stopped her from doing a healthy sprint.

'How dare you speak to me like that, you common sort of girrul!' Mrs Reid's voice was best Edinburgh-Morningside. Then, putting her hands together in a pleading gesture, she switched to a Highland singsong. 'Please don't put me away. Haff you no mercy?'

She steered a little to the side and leant against the wall for balance. The nurse moved to support her, ducking to avoid her patient's swipe.

'I'll show ye nay tae meddle wi' me, ye cat,' she cackled, then meekly she linked arms with the nurse. 'Aright, hen?'

'Yes. Let's go back to the ward,' said the nurse.

'All right.'

I'd never seen anything like it in my life. Unlike psychiatric nurses who were given nursing experience in a general hospital as part of their training, ours hadn't reciprocated. Mental health was such an unknown specialism I'm ashamed to admit that had Mrs Reid been bigger, I might have been scared of her. She'd recovered from her pneumonia, the Ross Memorial matron told us, but was now in Craig Dunain. I could see why. Physically, at least, she appeared to have fully recovered, but I couldn't imagine that she'd ever get back home again.

I assumed it would be different for Lorn.

After that visit, I drove to Chanonry Point. It's a spit of land between Fortrose and Rosemarkie and dabbles its feet in the Moray Firth.

Today, it's a mecca for tourists looking for dolphins leaping in the waters there, but in those distant days when they were all labelled porpoises the beach was a deserted spot. I'd go there sometimes and think about my patients, wondering if what I was doing was the best way to help them. The combination of the song of waves breaking on the shore, the sight of a wide sky and a sea which only spoke of freedom might not give an answer, but when I went home it was always with a clearer mind.

'This is my home. I don't want ever to leave here,' Lorn had said, looking round a ward where people were held fast in their beds. 'It's where I feel safe.'

No matter how hard I'd tried to convince her that there was a life outside the hospital walls, with people like Johnny to share their lives with her, she was adamant.

'Thanks for coming. I'll always remember you did that. But don't come back,' she said. 'You'd just remind me of another life I can't imagine me living now. It's not for the likes of me. I know I failed Johnny.' She looked at her bandaged wrists and shook her head. 'Poor bloke. I couldn't make him happy. But this is where I belong. The nurses are kind and nobody can touch me.' She hunched her back and turned to the wall.

I never knew her history. It might have been good to talk, but at the time I thought that Miss Macleod's new mantra on that theme was meant only for her staff.

As I wandered along the beach, Lorn's sad shadow stalked me until a leaping shape caught my eye. A porpoise? A sound like a creaking sail came from above. Looking up, I saw a swan flying in the direction of Inverness and wondered if it was heading home. Maybe I should do the same.

The next day promised to be a brighter one, especially as I'd be attending one of my newer patients. She made such light of a colostomy operation she was a joy to visit. It was disappointing that she hadn't fully recovered, but the skin surrounding the stoma had been refusing to heal.

She, however, was determinedly optimistic. After I'd visited a couple of times, she'd cried, 'Look! It's much better now. Thanks to your gentle touch and soothing cream, that awful red-raw area's on the mend. '

Like dear Mrs Henderson, she'd been far more interested in my life than hers. One day, she had fixed me with a bright gaze and mused, 'I used to know someone from your part of the world. He was a commercial traveller until he bought a hotel in Forres. He'd an unusual name for this part of the world, two sons and a daughter, and I'm sure one of them was called David.'

I grinned, fancying that the Fortrose nurse's home might provide better hospitality than Edinburgh's 29 Castle Terrace. Then I said, 'That's a coincidence. One of my good friend's families owns a hotel there. The name wouldn't be Yeadon, would it?'